In this journal, Tom Maxwell engages his grandson with life stories that resonate with both kids AND adults. With wit and example, Maxwell lifts the history and lore of America's greatest generation. It is great reading.

—Clyde G. Lear, Founder and retired President and Chairman of the Board, Learfield Communications.

This journal keeps you on the edge of your seat. It's exciting to read about Tom's captivating life and you feel like you are in the adventure with him. Tom is always on the cutting edge of life whether in military school, landing on an aircraft carrier or following Jesus. I was privileged to have pursued discipleship with this eager learner and man of faith. I observed how competitive Tom was as we ran along the Rhine River reviewing Bible verses.

—Paul Stanley, Senior Executive with the Navigators, teaching management skills world wide

I worked with Tom Maxwell on two cruises onboard the USS Oriskany CVA- 34, Detachment Golf, and in my twenty years of U.S. Naval Service, I have never respected another Naval officer so much, with the exception of Capt. Bill Laurentis who we both knew and admired equally. Tom was always in control, cool calm and collected no matter what emergency we were confronting. During the 1966/1967 cruises he experienced situations no one should be put into. I would follow this man into any military situation you could place us in. He is a gentlemen and an exceptional pilot. I can attest to all the above for I was there. Grandfather's Journal is a testimony to a life well lived and a must read for military and civilians alike. And I am blessed to have known both he and Betty since 1966.

—Ralph E. Estes III, USN, Senior Chief Petty Officer (RET)

Trent, thank you for persuading your Grandpa (Papa?) Maxwell to write his life story for you. Your grandparents have been among our very best friends since we first met in Bonn, Germany thirty-five years ago. Here is the well-told story of a man of integrity, who served his country for many years as a Naval officer. In his "retirement" years he developed a love for and personal ministry to incarcerated men and women as a volunteer with Prison Fellowship. When you and others need a compelling example of how to make life count in family, profession, community and the world, you need look no further than your very special Grandpa (Papa?) Maxwell.

—Bob Ehle, Special Representative, Global Aid Network
(the relief and development ministry of Cru)

Each generation produces leaders, great men and women of sacrifice and service who put the welfare of others ahead of their own pursuits. Grandfather's Journal tells the story of Tom Maxwell, a man who has led on every front. His service to his country and comrades is inspiring. His leadership in the home and community has launched new generations. His commitment to Christ, alongside his friend and fellow leader, Chuck Colson, has brought hope and life to thousands behind bars. Grandfather's Journal shows the way to make a difference throughout your life, across all divisions of men, in remarkable and unremarkable settings. A truly inspirational read.

—Dan Kingery, Prison Fellowship Ministries, Regional Leadership Team

In this journal, this voice…Tom Maxwell allows us passage within not just his life…but within his heart and mind. Tom encourages each of us to look within our own journey on this planet…to see if we are making excuses not to press through the pain and the ugly of this world…into the hope and love that dwells within being a disciple of Christ. Tom shares in a way that frees our hearts to believe that there is a remnant of hope. Tom is my Zoomie / Airedale brother and the honor is beyond words. Read, be consumed.

—Ron Gruber, Disciple of Christ…for Sons of Grace Mission

Grandfather's Journal

A Grandson's Journey into His Grandfather's Life

Journal of Captain Matthew Thomas Maxwell III, USN Retired
June 7, 1935 to December 28, 2013

TOM MAXWELL

WESTBOW°
PRESS
A DIVISION OF THOMAS NELSON
& ZONDERVAN

Print of EKA3B "Operation Wet Wing", by R.G. Smith, courtesy of www.rgsmithart.com
Author's picture, courtesy of Tracy Wrenn Crowe, Columbia, Missouri
Technical support, courtesy of A3 Skywarrior Association, www.a3skywarrior.com

Scriptures taken from the Holy Bible, New International Version®, NIV®. Copyright © 1973,
1978, 1984, 2011 by Biblica, Inc.™ Used by permission of Zondervan. All rights reserved
worldwide. www.zondervan.com The "NIV" and "New International Version" are trademarks
registered in the United States Patent and Trademark Office by Biblica, Inc.™ All rights reserved.

Scripture quotations taken from the New American Standard Bible®, Copyright
© 1960, 1962, 1963, 1968, 1971, 1972, 1973, 1975, 1977, 1995 by The
Lockman Foundation. Used by permission." (www.Lockman.org)

WestBow Press books may be ordered through booksellers or by contacting:

WestBow Press
A Division of Thomas Nelson & Zondervan
1663 Liberty Drive
Bloomington, IN 47403
www.westbowpress.com
1 (866) 928-1240

ISBN: 978-1-4908-5085-6 (sc)
ISBN: 978-1-4908-5086-3 (hc)
ISBN: 978-1-4908-5084-9 (e)

Library of Congress Control Number: 2014915951

Printed in the United States of America.

WestBow Press rev. date: 10/09/2014

Contents

Foreword

When my grandson asked me to write my journal of life, it was never my intention for *Grandfather's Journal* to become a book. It was only after spending a year writing this that I realized that it might be possible to share it with others besides my family. It is in no way spectacular—in my humble opinion, just a story of a blessed life where I was given the unique opportunity to serve first my country and then in a ministry to the least of these.

What would I pray that others might gain from reading this journal? First and foremost, I pray that there is a sovereign God who, two thousand years ago, offered us the unique opportunity to have a personal relationship with Him through the acceptance of His Son, Jesus. I am prayerfully hopeful that readers might find their way to the foot of the cross before age forty-two.

If you or members of your family are contemplating serving in the Armed Forces this journal might give real insight into what the self and family sacrifices are when you sign on for this honorable service. Although the sacrifices are great so are the rewards beyond what I could describe in this journal. God has blessed us to live in the most remarkable country in the history of the world and to be allowed to serve our nation is an honor beyond description.

Finally, I hope that the readers might catch a glimpse of what it is like to minister behind the walls and chain link fences to the "least of these" Once again, there are no words to describe the blessings of witnessing the life changes of the men and women who have stumbled and then met Jesus behind the walls—always with a realization that but for the grace of God go I. The brothers and sisters with whom you will minister are amazing members of the family of God. If for nothing more than the blessing of meeting Chuck Colson of Watergate fame and work with his prison fellowship team, this journey would have been worth all of the effort extended toward it.

My continued prayer is:

> Lord, guard and guide the men who fly
> And those who on the ocean ply;
> Be with our troops upon the land,
> And all who for their country stand:
> Be with these guardians day and night
> And may their trust be in thy might.
> —Author unknown, 1955

Acknowledgment

I would like to thank my Lord and Savior Jesus Christ for saving a wretch like me.

> Therefore, if anyone is in Christ, the new creation
> has come: The old has gone, the new is here.
> —2 Corinthians 5:17 (NIV)

Also deserving of thanks is my remarkable wife who, over fifty-seven years, not only led me to Christ but also provided awesome leadership while her sailor husband went to sea in ships, combat included. I am grateful as well for my blessed family, Matthew Thomas IV, Debra Ann, and Michael Louis, who also sacrificed for their country and supported mom at home.

Finally, I would like to thank Chuck Colson, a spiritual giant of a man who, through his book *Born Again*, helped Betty plant the seeds of redemption and then led me into a remarkably rewarding ministry to the least of these—a ministry that has lasted over thirty years and about which I can only say, "Praise the Lord."

Introduction

This journal was created at the request of Trent Michael Maxwell, the only grandson of the writer. Most of the journal was generated from stories shared with my grandson. I also hope to share this with my three special granddaughters: Meghann McKnight, Molly Waters, and Natasha Windsor Ruesing. Many of the memories are from my twenty-seven years as a naval aviator, including three years living in the Philippines immediately following World War II. The memories following my retirement from the navy in December 1982 reflect my continued Christian walk and my reluctant involvement in prison ministry.

CHAPTER 1

In the Beginning

I was born in Greenville, Tennessee, on June 7, 1935, to Matthew Thomas Maxwell II and Evelyn Bailes Maxwell. My father graduated as a civil engineer from the University of Alabama, and my mother graduated from Florence State Teachers College in Florence, Alabama. While living in Tennessee, my father was employed with the Civil Conservation Corps, a public works project. This started your grandfather's seminomadic life, as I lived in many places throughout my young life. My brother, Jess Bailes Maxwell, was born three years after me on April 19, 1938, three years before the Japanese bombed Pearl Harbor, starting World War II, the big war.

After the start of WWII, dad joined the US Army as a civil engineer. His first assignment was at the army's civil engineering base at Fort Belvoir, Virginia, just south of our nation's capital, Washington, DC. Although most of my childhood memories were of moving (I sometimes attended as many as three schools in one year), there are specific memories from several of the locations where we lived. At Fort Belvoir, we lived near the parade ground with woods behind our house; this was where we would go when the war sirens sounded. There were concrete bunkers where we would stay until the all-clear siren was sounded. At Fort Belvoir, I would go down to the parade field to watch the marching soldiers and bands. I think this may have been the beginning of my desire to serve in the military.

One day at school, I found out the army was going to bring an airplane to land on the parade field and give rides. So without telling my mom and dad (not a good idea), I went to the parade field and got my first airplane ride. I am sure this event increased my desire to be a pilot. When I got home, it was not fun; however, the exhilaration of my first ever airplane ride was more than worth the punishment.

After being at Fort Belvoir for a number of years, Dad chose to move into the Army Air Force (AAF); he became a civil engineer when the AAF became the US Air Force (USAF). One of the stations where we lived was Olmsted Field Air Force Base (AFB) in Middletown, Pennsylvania. Because we lived near the runway, I was able to see many USAF aircraft landing and taking off. I got to see one of the first B-29s bombers that were being used in WWII take off from that runway. I also remember playing on the parade field, driving a golf ball with a putter. The ball went through the window of the commanding general's car! For my dad, this was not a good thing—and nor was it good for me.

My First Overseas Travel and Reflections of Young Teenagers Living in the Philippine Islands, Which Had Just Been Ravaged by WWII

In 1946, following our tour of duty at Olmsted Field, my dad was transferred to Fort McKinley near Manila, Philippines. Since we were not allowed to travel with him, due to monetary reasons, we moved to my mother's home in Florence, Alabama. During that time, we lived with my mom's parents, the Bailes, whom the kids called Pal and Sweetie Pie. We also took time to visit my dad's father, Matthew Thomas Senior, and mother, in Tuscaloosa, Alabama, whom we called Boy-O-Boy and Sweet Thing. We also were able to visit my Aunt Auntie and Uncle Frank Malone, my mother's sister and her husband.

That year, there was a severe polio epidemic. I was twelve years old and Jess was nine, and Mom took us to the mountains, where we would be safer. It was in Florence that I met Johnny Archer, my lifetime best friend. You had the opportunity to meet Johnny the summer of 2014, when we had a remarkable reunion after more than 65 years in Florence. Johnny's parents owned a funeral home, and when I would spend the night with Johnny, he would always take me in the back door to where all the bodies were. One time he took me into the room with all the coffins, shut the door, and turned out the lights. I was scared stiff and know I did not sleep that night.

After more than a year apart, Mom and Dad had saved enough money to purchase passage for us to join Dad in the Philippines. We traveled on the USS *Marine Adder*, which was no luxury liner. Jess and I lived in a bunkroom and Mom in a stateroom with five other women. Almost the only time Jess and I saw Mom was during meals. We stopped shortly in Hawaii for fuel and then in Hong Kong to drop off about five hundred Chinese people traveling home after WWII. Shortly after we left Hawaii, a Chinese man committed suicide because he had lost his life's savings gambling in the bottom of the ship. They had to put his body where they stored the ice, and we did not have ice the rest of the voyage. It was a long two weeks to Hong Kong in hot weather without ice.

When we arrived in Hong Kong, the family of one of my dad's friends took us to dinner. As we drove through the streets, we were astonished to see so many children begging for a handout for food. This poverty was a side effect of the war that we had not experienced in America, and witnessing it made a big impact on my brother and me.

The Chinese family ordered chicken, and it came with a complete chicken standing up on the platter with brown rice beneath it. Neither Jess nor I could eat the chicken. After the family and Mom ate, they called their extended family to come and eat since food was in such short supply.

As we were preparing to leave Hong Kong, the family decided to purchase a camphor chest. From the top rail of our ship, we bargained with one of the many boats selling everything. We pulled the chest up to the deck of our ship using a rope; then, our traveling family put the money in a basket and sent it to the merchant's boat below. This chest now sits in your grandparent's bedroom.

We departed Hong Kong and headed for Manila, the capital of the Philippines. We had not seen Dad for over a year. When we were one day away from Manila, a USAF B-25 flew very low over our ship. Everyone went up to see it. We were totally shocked when on one pass Jess and I saw our dad waving at us from the side door of the plane! This only intensified our excitement to arrive and be with Dad.

The next day, as we sailed into Manila Bay we had our first glimpse of how ravaged the Philippine Islands had been by WWII. We could not believe the number of sunken ships sitting on the bottom of the bay. These were the ships that had been bombed as the Americans took back the Philippines from the Japanese. We passed by Fort Drum, a cement ship built by the Japanese in the middle of the harbor to protect Manila Bay. We also passed by Corregidor Island, where General McArthur was forced to leave the Philippines and gave the famous quote "I shall return."

None of these historical sights brought the same excitement as seeing the customs boat come along side to inspect our cargo. Then, we saw dad on the boat boarding the *Marine Adder* to ride the last leg of a long journey to the pier with us. Wow! What a reunion we had! After we had been away from our father for over a year, it was so special to once again be a family, even if we were thousands of miles from our homeland. I vividly remember Dad hugging Mom and looking down at his two sons with tears of joy in his eyes.

We lived for one year at an old Philippine Army base called Fort McKinley, the Japanese had occupied during the war. My dad had left the air force and was working for the Manila Engineering District (MANED), helping to rebuild Manila. Each day, we rode the school bus for an hour to the American school in Manila with an armed guard on the bus. Following the war, there remained a terrorist group on Luzon Island called the Hucks. They had been known to stop school buses and kidnap children for ransom. I am sure that is why we traveled daily with Philippine Army soldiers on our bus, and I know that even though Mom would take us to the bus every morning, she never got used to seeing armed guards protecting her young children.

I have many vivid memories of the year we lived in our small, two-bedroom house at Fort McKinley. Behind our house was a jungle with some paths cut through the trees, and beneath our house was a maze of tunnels the Japanese had dug to protect themselves during the bombings by US airplanes. Jess and I were forbidden by our parents to enter the tunnels, so, of course, we explored them! We found a tunnel from our house to the swimming pool, which was about a mile away. When Dad and Mom found out, there was trouble in the house for two young boys. What we had not known was that there were many unexploded bombs in the tunnels that had not been cleared. The tunnels were actually very dangerous. Dad said we had been fortunate to get to the swimming pool in one piece. Near the exit from the cave to the swimming pool one day, we found a white ball about the size of a softball, but heavier. Wanting to know what was inside, we threw it against a concrete wall, but nothing happened. We later learned that it was a tank grenade, designed to explode and destroy any tank that ran over it—another close call and a valuable lesson learned. Following our move from McKinley, Dad found out that a demolition team had found a two-thousand-pound live bomb under the road behind our house.

Tunnels and leftover bombs were not the only dangers on the island. Our neighbor woke up one morning to find a twelve-foot python curled up in a chair in his living room. After some work with a 45-caliber pistol, the snake was dead, but our neighbor's living room was a mess. Another day, while Jess and I were exploring a jungle path behind our house, we ran into a nest of baby snakes. We poked it with a stick, and, although very small, the snakes rose up, their heads spread like hoods. We were smart enough to know that they were cobras, one of the most poisonous snakes in the world. If the mom snake had returned and bitten us, we would have most likely died.

After a year at Fort McKinley, dad was transferred to Clark Air Force Base on Central Luzon Island, about two hours north of Manila. We lived in a green, wood-frame house that had been built on stilts to keep the house from flooding when the typhoons came. It had a tin roof, so the house was very loud when it rained. Jess and I slept in one bedroom, and Mom and Dad had another. There were servant's quarters in the back of the house where Daniel Soriano and his wife lived. I do not remember how much they received in pay, but it was not much. Once you bond with Filipino people, they are very loyal, and Daniel was no exception. He was devoted to my parents and watched out for Jess and me. One night while we were coming home from a movie, some of the bigger boys stole my pants. I then had to go home embarrassed and in my shorts. When Daniel, our house boy, found out, he headed out the door to take care of those kids. Dad had to stop him before Daniel hurt them.

Across the street from our house were the large, concrete homes where senior officers lived. When a bad typhoons came, we would go to these homes for protection. Each typhoon has three stages: the front, the eye, and then the back. When the eye arrives, there is dead silence with no wind at all, but when the back of the typhoon comes, it is usually more dangerous than the front.

Late one night during the eye of a typhoon, Jess and I thought the storm was over and went out to look at all the damage. Walking toward the parade field, we suddenly saw military police (MP) cars everywhere. Guess who they were looking for! When Dad realized we had walked outside, he immediately called the MPs. We were returned safely to the general's quarters and a frantic mother just before the back of the storm hit.

The parade ground we had been walking toward was very long, about the length of two football fields, with one giant tree in the middle. One day, a classmate asked me to help him with a project that evening. He came by the house around nightfall and we proceeded to the tree standing in the middle of the parade ground. When we got there, I realized he had stolen some gunpowder and made a pipe bomb with a fuse in it—like a firecracker. I warned him that if he set off the bomb we would get in serious trouble. To my dismay, he put the bomb under the tree and lit the fuse. We took off like scared rabbits, and when we reached the road around the parade field, the bomb went off and blew up the tree. We were both so scared we ran and hid under his house for almost two hours. Once again, there were MPs all over the base looking for whoever set off the bomb. I ran home through a back alley, and no one ever discovered who had blown up the tree. Years later, I admitted to my mom and dad what had happened, and they told me that if my friend and I had been caught, we could have been locked up.

Another time Jess and I and several of our friends went to the Bam Bam River, a river that was about two miles from where we lived. The river was fairly fast moving and crystal clear, and the water was very cold. Since it was one hundred degrees, we knew it would feel great. Since it was just us boys, we decided to go skinny-dipping. We took off our clothes and found a bend in the river that had a good curve and slower-moving water, and we had a ball swimming for about an hour. Returning to where we started, we found that our clothes were gone and all that remained were our jockey shorts. In the distance, we saw some Filipino boys headed our way and presumed they were returning to steal what we had left. We then rushed to at least retrieve our shorts so we would not have to return home naked.

There we were, in the late afternoon, with only our underwear to wear. We needed badly to get home and avoid getting in trouble, but we were too embarrassed to walk home in broad daylight in only our jockey shorts. One of the older boys suggested that we wait until nightfall and then try to sneak home. This was the plan we chose. While we were walking home, our friendly MPs found us, put us in a police van, and delivered us home to some very frightened and unhappy parents.

Life in the Philippines after WWII had very real dangers, and not everyone was as lucky as Jess and I had been. Two of our neighbor friends found a butterfly bomb device in the jungle behind our houses. Acting like most inquisitive young boys would, they got their father's hammer and screwdriver and attempted to find out what was inside the butterfly bomb. It exploded, killing them both. The next week in school we spent an entire day with a demolition expert, who showed us what to never touch or pick up. This was when Jess and I learned that the ball we had thrown against the wall while living at Fort McKinley was a tank bomb.

Another memory about the dangers of the Philippines involved the Negrito tribe that lived near the base. During the war, the Japanese referred to them as "black death" since they had killed so many Japanese soldiers with their bow and arrows. The leader of this tribe was Colonel Laxamana, who had become a good friend of my dad's because my dad had given the Negrito tribe a lot of material to rebuild their village buildings. Colonel Laxamana had his own jeep and driver and had been given the honorary rank of lieutenant colonel.

One evening, Dad saw some of the Negritos stealing wood from a project Dad was in charge of. The next time Dad saw the colonel, he told him that he would work to get whatever the colonel needed, but he did not want members of the tribe stealing materials from active work sites. Weeks later when dad saw the colonel again, he thanked him for stopping the stealing of the material. Colonel Laxamana told dad that it would never happen again, because he had killed both men involved. Dad was deeply saddened when he found this out and said he would not have told him if he had known that it would result in such a harsh penalty for the men. However, there was never anything else stolen while we were at Clark AFB.

It was also at Clark that Jess and I started to learn how to be young businessmen. We found that, unlike in the States, we as teenagers could sell beer in the Philippines. So on Saturday and Sunday, we would set up a beer and soda stand on the ninth hole of the Clark golf course and refresh the thirsty golfers. They deeply appreciated it, and Jess and I made our first serious dollars.

In spite of the dangers, the Philippines was a paradise for young boys. I have to believe that even when I was a child, someone was watching over me. After three years in the Philippines, Dad rejoined the air force as a colonel and was transferred to the Strategic Air Command (SAC) headquarters in Omaha, Nebraska, as the head civil engineer, working for the infamous Gen. Curtis Lemay. Prior to leaving, we drove to Manila and stayed in officers' quarters as we awaited our flight back to the United States.

Dad was deeply appreciated for the work he had done in the Philippines, and the night before our departure, there was a big party for Mom, Dad, and family at the officers' club. As a departing gift, Mr. Benny Lim, a Chinese businessman, gave my dad a beautiful Philippine mahogany desk that had once been used in Malacanang Palace by the president of the Philippines. Later research on the desk, which is currently in Grandfather's den, showed that President Sergio Osmena, the first president of the Philippines following WWII, had used it as well. In fact, President Osmena walked ashore with Gen. Douglas McArthur at Leyte Gulf during his triumphant return to the Philippines on October 20, 1944.

Following the farewell party, we all moved into the main ballroom, where everyone was playing bingo. Mom won a cash gift, and then the final round was a cover-your-board game, the prize a beautiful handmade set of twelve place settings of Chinese china painted with colorful chickens. Who won the chicken china but your teenage grandfather? Since I had a girlfriend, Barbie, I traded the china to my mother for a set of pearls that I could give to her. Later, after I was married, my mother returned the china to us, and today it sits quietly in the china cabinet. The day after the farewell party, we departed Manila, by a propeller transport, stopping at several islands in the Pacific on our way home.

CHAPTER 2

Returning Home to the United States

Our family purchased a house in Bellevue, Nebraska, just outside Omaha. In 1949, I started my freshman year at Bellevue High School. Coming from an overseas government school, being a freshman, and not knowing my classmates made for a most difficult school year. This prompted Mom and Dad to enroll me in Kemper Military School in Boonville, Missouri. Although my "new boy" year was difficult, Kemper and the discipline were just what your grandfather needed. I stayed at the school during the year and returned home for breaks and summer. My summers at home were filled with work at the Offutt Air Force Base Officers' Club and later for Peter Kiewit and Sons Construction Company, where I did manual labor and decided that I did not want to do this kind of work my entire life.

I started my junior year at KMS as a platoon sergeant; later that year I was promoted to cadet lieutenant and platoon commander. I was thriving at Kemper. I was also selected to head up Kemper's first crack drill platoon, the Kemper Guardsmen, which was great because we had the honor of performing all over Missouri. I was on the KMS football, track, tennis, and swimming teams. My senior year I won first place in the state for the hundred-yard butterfly with a time slower than high school students on my younger son's (your dad's) swim team in Annandale, Virginia.

In my senior year at Kemper, I was promoted to company commander and to the rank of cadet captain. I also would meet the most beautiful girl in Boonville, who was the drum major for the BHS band. In the fall of 1952, I asked her to be my date to the Camp Perry dance, and she accepted. On our first date, I got back to Kemper late and had to climb the fire escape to the third floor of D barracks so I would not get caught breaking curfew. Betty Ann Dowling was like most of the young ladies at BHS and enjoyed the Kemper dances, especially the yearly military ball, where there would always be a nationally known dance band. During the military ball, the balcony of the Johnston Field House, which is now the YMCA, was always packed with Boonville citizens who wanted to hear the band and watch the glorious grand march. My brother, Jess, joined me in his junior year and graduated from Kemper high school.

I returned to Kemper Junior College in the fall of 1953 for my freshman year of college and was promoted to lieutenant colonel and assistant corps commander. The second-year college student who had been selected to be corps commander turned down the job because he was a pre-med major and felt it would be too difficult to do both. Much to my surprise, I was the first college freshman in Kemper history asked to become the corps commander. I continued to date the most beautiful girl in Boonville, who would one day become my wife and your grandmother, and some would say I was totally smitten.

As the corps commander, I had many more privileges than the other cadets, and the leeway led to some mischief. Although I could most likely write a book on the pranks we played on each other at Kemper, one I remember particularly well. One Sunday evening, the battalion health officer, Herb Kaufman, and his roommate had dates in Columbia. While they were gone, we moved their entire room into the joint bathroom used by all the senior staff, beds and all. When reveille sounded each morning, we had ten minutes to dress and be in formation on the Kemper court. Reveille sounded at six on the Monday morning after our prank, and we rolled out of our beds only to find the bathroom door locked. Thirty minutes later, a very embarrassed senior staff showed up for breakfast with very red faces.

Between my freshman and sophomore years, I attended Army Reserve Officer Training Corps (ROTC) summer camp at Fort Meade, in Maryland. At the end of my freshman year, I also applied for entrance to West Point but was not accepted. While at Fort Mead, I used all the money I had made to buy an engagement ring to give to Betty Ann when I returned to Boonville. I remember first asking Mr. Dowling if I could marry his daughter when we finished college, and he graciously said yes. I then asked Betty to come upstairs to her bedroom because I had a gift for her. In her bedroom, I gave her the ring and asked her to marry me. What an incredible day it was when she said yes! We both realized the next two years would be very difficult since she was in pre-nursing at Christian College in Columbia and I had two more years of college. During my sophomore year at Kemper, the Military Department did not know what to do with me because I had already been corps commander. They decided to make me a tactical officer, and I received a single room, which was very special.

During my sophomore year, I also embarked on my second private entrepreneurial endeavor. Following dinner, there was nightly study hall that lasted until 10:00 p.m. After study hall, we had thirty minutes of free time until lights-out to get ready for the following day's duties. Since our meals were not always the best, I hired a cadet to go around to each room and take orders for hamburgers and cheeseburgers to be delivered at ten, when study hall was over. Nemo's, which was about three blocks from the school, was delighted to provide this service. Promptly at ten, the runners would meet Nemo in front of the school and would then have all the burgers delivered by ten after. When I headed home for Christmas, I could not believe we had made over $500, which, in 1954, was a lot of money. Additionally, Betty and I were able to attend many functions that year since she was in nearby Columbia. This included attending, with my parents, my graduation from Kemper and commissioning as a second lieutenant in the army.

In the fall of 1955, I entered Missouri University in Columbia as an engineering student. In order to graduate in two years, I took twenty-three credit hours, but I also foolishly pledged to be in the ATO fraternity. Classes, the fraternity, and drives to and from St. Louis to see my future wife, who was then studying nursing at Washington

University, did not work. Halfway through the semester, with my college world falling apart, I visited the air force recruiter to see if I could go to flight school since I had always wanted to fly. At the time, the AF did not have pilot vacancies, but he offered to let me enlist and wait for a slot to open for me to attend flight school. I asked what would happen if, when the slot opened, I was not physically qualified. He responded that I would spend four years as an enlisted man. This obviously did not make much sense for someone who already had an army commission.

As I dejectedly left the office, a navy chief petty officer across the room said, "Son, would you like to fly airplanes?" After a three-week period of processing, I was headed to Pensacola, Florida, for navy flight school as a naval aviation cadet (NAVCAD).

CHAPTER 3

Off to Serve My Country

I arrived at the naval air station (NAS) in Pensacola, Florida, as a member of the last class of 1955 which was the 43rd class of 1955, and was very excited for my future. The excitement lasted until I ran into my first Marine Corps drill sergeant, who was standing one inch in front of my face yelling about how worthless I was. Welcome to NAVCAD boot camp. Needless to say, I was more than ready to get a short leave to go home for Christmas, which I split between my parents' home in Bellevue, Nebraska, and visiting Betty in Boonville. After sharing my difficult time in boot camp with Betty's mom, she told me, "If you don't like it, just come home," not realizing I had signed a four-year commitment.

To be very honest, I was not sure I wanted to return, since I had to face my friendly drill sergeant again. I still had five more weeks of boot camp training—a 5:00 a.m. wakeup call for exercise and drill, classes all day, and the obstacle course in the afternoon. My military training from Kemper helped, and I was soon promoted to platoon leader, which gave me more freedom. Despite the difficulties, I continued, because I knew now that I wanted to become a naval aviator.

After an intense eight weeks, I found myself at Saufley Field learning to fly the T-34 aircraft, which was very exciting. After about ten flights, my instructor told me to land in a farmer's field. He got out of the plane we were in and told me, "Do not forget to come back and pick me up." I was just as excited as afraid as I taxied to the end of the field for takeoff. Once airborne, I could not believe that for the first time I was flying by myself, or soloing. I did not forget to return and pick up my instructor, and he was very complimentary of my flying skills. I returned to my base and put on my uniform only to have my classmates cut my navy blue tie in half—a sign that one had soloed. What an extremely exciting day for your grandfather!

After completing my primary flying, I reported to Baron Field, where I learned to fly the T-28 for instrument (in clouds) and formation flying. Formation flying was a blast, and instrument flying was difficult. While at Baron Field, I completed my first cross-country, a flight to another base one hundred miles from my home base, alone, and returned safely. I had wanted to fly to St. Louis to see my fiancée and the place where I had joined the Navy, but my instructor said no way. So I did what only a lovesick future naval aviation cadet would foolishly do: I drove seven hundred miles to St. Louis. I left at noon on Friday, arrived in St. Louis at midnight, and slept for four hours. At noon on Saturday, I picked up your grandmother, and we had a glorious twelve hours together before I told her good-bye and headed back to Pensacola. I arrived late Sunday afternoon, completely exhausted and certainly in no shape to fly the next day. I often remember this when I challenge our kids not to drive so far in one day.

In the summer of 1956, I reported to Foley Field for the most demanding part of my training: carrier qualifications. I had to first learn to fly the SNJ aircraft and then prepare to go to the carrier. Before going to the ship, we were required to fly twenty field carrier landing practice (FCLP) flights, where the landing signal officer (LSO) would evaluate each landing. We would fly a racetrack pattern at five hundred feet just like we would do at the ship. For me, this four-month training was the most difficult flying I had done and more dangerous than any other. During my thirteenth or fourteenth flight, we were ordered to immediately land and taxi to our parking area. As I taxied in, I knew that something very bad had happened, since I could see black smoke rising from the area we had been flying over. Once out of the aircraft and back in the ready room (or briefing room), we were told that two of the six aircraft in our flying pattern had collided. Both planes had crashed, and both students were dead.

I returned to my barracks that night in complete shock. For the first time, I thought about quitting. I did not want to call my parents and Betty Ann, for I knew it would also make them very fearful. Knowing that we needed a break, the navy gave all four remaining students a four-day pass. I immediately left for St. Louis to see Betty Ann and discuss my future. I cannot tell you what an encouragement your grandmother was to me, as were my parents. I returned to Pensacola with renewed determination to complete my flight training.

We finished our training on D-Day. In the ready room, four prospective carrier aviators were briefing for our six landings on the USS *Saipan* in Pensacola Bay. All four pilots were scared straight; you could've cut the air with a knife. Not one of us mentioned that there were four, not six, planes going to the carrier, but I know that each pilot could not help but notice those who were missing. We headed out to maintenance for our aircraft assignment and then to our assigned aircraft. We were wished well by our plane captain, started our engines, taxied out, and lined up, waiting for clearance. All four pilots took off, joined up in formation, and headed for the USS *Saipan*. At a point twenty miles from the carrier, the lead aircraft checked in with the ship and was given permission to break and land. With our hearts in our throats, we prepared for our very first carrier landing.

The exhilaration of my first carrier landing is most difficult to describe, but there I was. As I prepared to launch for my second landing, a plane captain jumped up on my wing and asked if my radio was working, and I said that it was. I launched for my second landing, and I turned downwind and heard the tower call one of the aircraft, whose pilot would not answer. Again, after my second landing, the plane captain climbed on my wing to ask if my radio worked before I took off.

Six landings later, I headed home with the biggest smile on my face ever, wondering why someone had climbed up on my wing during each landing to ask if my radio worked. I landed, taxied in, parked, and shut down, and when met by my plane captain, I told him about the unanswered radio calls I had heard. It was then that we both discovered what had happened. When crews recently repainted the numbers on our aircraft, they changed the numbers on the nose that the ship control tower could see but did not change the number on the wing that I could see. So when the tower called the number on the nose, I did not answer, since I thought it was one of the other aircraft.

Although I had asked for single engine training for my advanced phase, I was selected for multiengine training at NAS Hutchinson in Kansas. I had a glorious Christmas vacation with my family and your grandmother before reporting to NAS Hutchinson. We realized how much better it would be for me to be in Kansas, not Texas, where I would have never been able to drive to St. Louis to see my future wife.

The first aircraft that I flew at Hutchinson was the S2F, a carrier based antisubmarine warfare aircraft. The S2F was a twin-engine propeller aircraft with two sets of controls, one for the pilot and one for the copilot. During the first phase of my training, the instructor could fly in the right seat. Following five flights and a "safe for solo" check, we were allowed to fly solo with another student. For my solo cross-country, I again asked to fly to St. Louis to see my future bride, but my instructor, Lt. Cdr. "Spender" Collins, asked me if I would fly to Travis City, Michigan. I would later find out that the reason for the trip was that my instructor was a gambler and had lost all of his family's money in card games. His father was the president of a bank, and my instructor was going home to borrow money to support his family. His parents were very gracious to me but not to their son. I found out that I was not the first student to make his cross-country to Travis City. Needless to say, I received a very good grade on my cross-country.

The second navy aircraft I trained in was a land-based, anti-submarine warfare aircraft. The P2V was bigger than what I had previously flown and also a twin-engine propeller aircraft. During this phase of training, we also had the difficult task of learning to navigate. We had to memorize all of the stars for shooting with a sextant so that we could shoot lines of bearings to use for navigation. We also had to memorize Morse code. We flew several flights at night with the instructor flying and the students navigating with a sextant and the stars. I only got lost one time, shooting the wrong star. Our overwater flight, where we had no landmarks to help us, was to Panama City, Panama. This was also the longest flight I had ever flown and my first flight into a foreign country.

Again, after five flights and a certification of "safe for solo," we took the aircraft, each of us flying with another student. My solo cross-country was to Olathe Naval Air Station in Olathe, Kansas, near Kansas City.

Grandmother Betty was in nursing school at Washington University School of Nursing in St. Louis, and we were able to visit each other often. Several months before Christmas, we both realized that since Betty did not graduate until June and I would receive my Navy wings in April, the only time we could get married was over Christmas. Our parents were not too happy, but on December 28, 1956, we were married at the Nelson Memorial United Methodist Church in Boonville, Missouri, in a small wedding. Our reception dinner was at the Fredrick Hotel, and we went to Kansas City for our honeymoon. Fifty-seven years after our wedding, on December 28, 2013, your cousin Natasha also was married at the Nelson Memorial UMC.

Early in January, after a short honeymoon in Kansas City, I returned to complete my flight training, and Grandmother returned to her nurses training in St. Louis. That month I received my first orders to join utility squadron one (VU-1) at Naval Air Station Barbers Point in Hawaii. Most of my classmates received orders to Guam, but your grandmother and I were overjoyed at the thought of going to Hawaii. VU-1 had many different kinds of aircraft, including jets, which I hoped someday to fly. On April 2, 1957, my father, Col. M. T. Maxwell Senior (Pops), pinned on my navy wings of gold. What an incredibly proud day that was! I left shortly for St. Louis to see Grandmother Betty since I knew we would be separated for several months until she graduated in June.

CHAPTER 4

Joining the Fleet

When it was time to report to VU-1, I flew out of Andrews AFB in California and landed at the Honolulu Airport in Hawaii. A wonderful family from VU-1 welcomed me with, of course, flower leis, and then I was taken to the bachelor officer quarters (BOQ) at Barbers Point. I was very excited to report to my squadron the next day. My first assignment was as the squadron first lieutenant. This meant I was responsible for the squadron upkeep and housing. I was told that, since I had come out of multiengine flight school, I would first learn to fly what the navy called the jig dog (JD), which was an air force B-26. The mission of the aircraft was to pull targets behind the aircraft so that the navy ships could conduct firing practice at the sleeve behind the plane. The second aircraft that I checked out in was the single-engine F6F fighter called the Hellcat. Wow, was it fun to fly!

We had blue F6s and red F6s. We used the aircraft as drones so that the carrier-based jet fighters could shoot missiles at the aircraft. The blue aircraft were the control aircraft and the red the drone. We would fly the drone with no pilot from a box in our aircraft like one would with a radio-controlled model. On the wingtips of the drones were flares that we would ignite so that heat-seeking missiles would hit the flares and not the airplane. Usually this worked well, but on one afternoon, something went very wrong. A drone wingtip had been hit that morning, and that F6 would not fly straight; instead, it would turn slightly, putting the control aircraft we were in directly in the flight path of the missile. Suddenly we heard the fighter pilot who had fired the missile screaming, "Hellcats, break right! The missile is headed for your aircraft." We both turned hard to the right, and the missile passed over my canopy, barely missing me. The missile did not explode, and I could now breathe again.

The other exciting thing that happened while I was flying the F6 was that several of us got to fly in the movie *South Pacific* during the raid on Pearl Harbor. In that scene, the Japanese were flying through a channel prior to the bombing. Following a new paint job to make our F6Fs to look like Japanese zero aircraft, we were launched to fly in formation down the channel for this scene. Following the flight, we were all treated to a lunch with the beautiful blond lead actress Mitzi Gaynor. She was very kind to us and thanked us for serving our country. The only unhappy member of our team was Lieutenant Commander Conner since the painters demoted him to the rank of ensign.

During the months before Betty joined me in Hawaii, I learned to surf. I also found a fully furnished two-bedroom house on the beach; we could walk out our back door and into the Pacific Ocean. After your grandmother graduated, I excitedly booked her on the cruise ship *Lalani* from San Francisco to Hawaii. Mom and Dad (Pops and MeMe) drove to San Francisco to meet Betty and put her safely on the ship. There was one very excited man waiting for her with three beautiful flower leis to put around her neck when she arrived five days later in Honolulu. Even knowing what a wonderful cook your grandmother is today, I must admit that on the one-hour trip to our first home together, I asked her what we were having for supper, and she turned white. She told me she could not even open a can of soup! A great navy friend and neighbor, Faye Ward, helped teach Betty how to cook.

I can only describe our days in that beach home as glorious, but we would move three more times in the three years we were in Hawaii. The beach house was thirty minutes from the naval air station at Barbers Point; with only one car, the distance was challenging.

In my position as first lieutenant, I was in charge of the naval defense platoon (NDP). My job was to make the men march—which sailors do not like to do—and learn to use their weapons. I presented them with the opportunity to become a crack drill team like the Kemper Guardsmen, and the men loved it! We jazzed up their uniforms and had their rifles plated with chrome. Over time, not only was there a waiting list to become a VU-1 Guardsman, but the group also became known throughout the islands.

Betty, wanting to use the skills she had learned in nursing school, applied for a job at the hospital of the Eva Sugarcane Plantation. With the job, we were offered plantation housing, which was inexpensive and near the hospital and the base. It was a one-bedroom, fix-it-up apartment (that your dad has seen), and it needed badly to be refurbished. Years later, when our youngest son, Michael, saw the apartment, he could not believe his parents had once lived there.

Betty became pregnant with our first child, and we were very excited! Realizing that the one bedroom apartment was not big enough for a new arrival, we moved to a nearby village, Eva Beach, where we found another two-bedroom house on the beach. During this time, my dad received orders to report to the Pacific Air Force Command at Hickam AFB in Hawaii, about thirty minutes from where we lived. Haveing my mom and dad so close was special, and ended up being very important.

During a seven-month checkup for Grandmother's pregnancy with Matt, she told the doctor at the Kapiolani hospital in Honolulu that she was having problems; he told her it was false labor. On the way back to our home, we stopped at my mom and dad's house at Hickam AFB. After Grandmother described her condition to my mom, she told me to immediately take her back to the hospital, which I did.

Matthew Thomas Maxwell IV was born a few hours later, on January 5, 1959, two months premature. Weighing just two pounds, Matt was very sick and was put into an incubator to help with his breathing. Two days later, the doctors told us that they had done all they could and that our son would most likely not live. That evening, I went to the base chapel, got down on my knees, and asked a God I did not know to save Matt's life. The next day, the doctor called and told us that during the night our son had taken a turn for the better and would most likely live. Ten long weeks later, we brought Matt home. His wonderful mother would not leave his side as she nursed him to full health. The only time she left him was when your grandfather made her go to a movie with a girlfriend. When she anxiously returned home and found out that grandfather had fed him the wrong baby food, and was very unhappy.

I was a trained naval aviator, and after two years, I wanted to go aboard a carrier. The navy agreed and transferred me to Air Anti-Submarine Squadron Thirty-Seven (VS-37) to fly the S2F I had flown in flight school. The squadron was located at the Los Alamitos Naval Air Station near Los Angeles, California.

CHAPTER 5

Going to Sea

In VS-37, I was assigned to the maintenance department as the line officer. Betty and I rented a house near the base in Stanton, California. Being in an operational squadron was great, and I looked forward to making my first landings on the carrier USS *Hornet*, on which we would deploy. The work and hours were long but very rewarding.

After about six months in California, Betty became pregnant with our daughter, Debra. Nine months later it was time for Debra to arrive. I headed to the hospital only for Betty, a nurse, to tell me that we should go by the doctor's office first. Nervously, I objected, but Betty insisted. At the doctor's office, she was seen immediately. Shortly thereafter, the doctor emerged and asked how fast I could drive—Debra's arrival was imminent. How I kept from getting a ticket I do not know, but we just made it to the hospital. A beautiful girl, Debra Ann Maxwell, was born on February 9, 1960, in Long Beach. As with Matt, Betty did an awesome job of taking care of her.

Our workups had begun for our six-month deployment on the USS *Hornet.* Just before deploying, we put our furniture in storage and prepared for Betty, Debra, and Matt to return to Boonville during my six-month cruise. After I put my entire family on the airplane in Los Angeles with large tears in my eyes, I drove back to the base, determined to never do this again—it was too emotionally difficult. The next week, I submitted my resignation from the navy, stating that my reason for leaving was to return to college and obtain my degree. I was well aware that I would have to complete my six-month cruise before leaving the navy.

One week before departing on the USS *Hornet*, I received a call from a Commander Rippy at the Pentagon in Washington. He said, "Lieutenant Maxwell, I was just processing your request for resignation and noticed that the reason you were leaving the navy was to attend college."

"Yes, sir," I answered.

Commander Rippy then informed me that I had been selected to attend the Naval Postgraduate School in Monterey, California, to receive my bachelor's degree, which he'd wanted me to know before he processed the resignation. Shocked, I asked if I could call him back. After at least a two-hour conversation with Betty, we both decided that it would be foolish, with two young children, to turn down a free two-year college education, while being paid a rather good salary. I then called Commander Rippy, thanked him for taking time to call me and let me know of my selection, and told him I would be officially withdrawing my resignation. My maintenance officer, Commander Stanley, was very pleased with my decision.

The cruise was busy and exciting, and with so much work to be done, the time passed very quickly. Our first stop was in Hawaii at Pearl Harbor, near where Mom and Dad lived. Since Dad was still on active duty, I was able to take him flying in the S2F and show him what we did. It was great fun, and he was most impressed, even if my air force dad thought his son was in the wrong service. However, although I could not have known it, this was the last time I would see my mother (MeMe), since she would pass away at the young age of 48 while I was on cruise. Thus the Hawaii visit holds a lot of sad memories.

The USS *Hornet* also stopped in Japan, Hong Kong, and the Philippines. While in Subic Bay, Philippines, I was able to fly back to Clark AFB and visit where I had lived as a child. I was able to see our old house and the swimming pool and officers' club—and no, there was still no tree in the middle of the parade ground. I looked for our servant, Daniel Soriano, and was saddened when I could not find information on him. However, the visit did bring back many good memories from my days in 1948.

The flying off the carrier was demanding and we were involved in many antisubmarine warfare exercises and even were able to track a Russian submarine. While in VS-37, I logged a total of 580 hours in the S2F with forty-nine night flights. I had 134 carrier landings, sixty-four at night. I remember having a problem only one time.

One dark night during a mission, I was the pilot in the left seat, and my copilot, Lt. Bill Grimm, was in the copilot's seat. When flying at night over water, you must totally depend on your flight instruments to tell you what the altitude of the aircraft is. The principal instrument that measures this is your gyro horizon. In the instrument is a little airplane, and when you turn, the little plane turns just like the airplane. The pilot has one, and the copilot has a backup that works off a different system. On one black night, mine had gone out, but the off flag, which should tell you it is not working, did not come down, so I assumed it was working. When Bill observed my erratic flying, he took the aircraft from me and safely landed the aircraft back on the ship from the right seat, which was very difficult. If he had not taken control of the aircraft, there is no question we would have flown into the water.

After six months, we returned home, and I immediately got in my automobile and headed for Boonville with a shipmate from St. Louis. We drove without stopping. What a wonderful reunion when I arrived home to my precious wife and children, all of whom wondering who this strange man was. As promised by the Bureau of Naval Personnel, we were transferred to The Naval Post Graduate School in Monterey, California.

CHAPTER 6

Off to Shore Duty and Back to School and a Joint Staff Tour

During our time in Monterey, we lived in a small three-bedroom apartment in crowded navy housing. My studies were in naval engineering, and I spent most of my time studying. The Naval Postgraduate School is on a beautiful old campus and employed very smart professors who knew that, unless we wanted to hurt our career, we needed to pass—so they were not easy on the students.

Wanting to stay in good physical shape, I foolishly turned out for six-man tackle football. This was a large mistake. On our first road trip, to the Naval Air Station Lemoore, we took the field with fourteen players, and Naval Air Station Lemoore showed up with fifty. That afternoon was one of the longest of my life, and the ride home seemed just as long. I only remember that the score was something like fifty-five to zero. When I returned to the school, I contacted a Lieutenant Eisenhower, who had been an all-American football player while attending the Naval Academy, and asked him if he would join us. He politely told me that there was no way he would join the team. I am sure he knew a lot more about six-man football than I did. We did not go to a bowl, and as a matter of fact, I don't think we won one game. Your grandmother, Betty, was sure I had lost my mind.

While at school, as aviators we were required to fly four hours a month to stay proficient. I was very excited when I found out that I would be able to check out in the T2J single-engine jet. This was my first navy jet to fly, and it was great. After the required period of time, I became qualified to check other pilots out in the aircraft.

On one mission, I was in the front seat checking out another pilot. As we were returning to the naval air facility over Monterey Valley, I accidentally hit the canopy release handle, and the canopy was ejected from the aircraft. Thankfully, it landed in a farmer's field and did no damage, but there was one more problem. In every cockpit, there is a handle that has two positions: one position allows each pilot to eject separately, and the other enables the instructor pilot to eject both pilots out of the aircraft. In this aircraft, the handle was in the wrong position, and if the student in the back seat had ejected, your grandfather would have also been ejected, and we would have lost the airplane. When the canopy released, the student pilot thought I had ejected and reached for the ejection handle. Thankfully, he heard me on the radio declaring an emergency and asking to immediately land. Realizing I was still in my seat, the student did not pull the ejection handle, and I landed the aircraft with no other problems. We were met by several fire trucks and escorted to the flight line.

When I completed school the following June, I wanted to return to flying but was told I must complete another shore assignment. My dad had been stationed at the North American Air Defense (NORAD) command in Colorado Springs before his assignment to the Pacific Air Forces in Hawaii, and he advised me that there were navy billets at the headquarters in Colorado. I called, and there was a billet for a navy lieutenant on the joint staff with the NORAD Space Detection and Tracking System (SPADATS). I was told this joint staff assignment would be good for my career, and I accepted the position.

Reflections of a Young Naval Officer Serving on a Joint Staff

After completing engineering school in Monterey, I arrived as a young lieutenant with my family in Colorado Springs, very excited about my new job. I was the only naval officer on the North American

Air Defense Command (NORAD) Space Detection and Tracking System (SPADATS) staff. I served with two air force officers and one army officer. Our mission was to monitor everything that was in space just above the atmosphere. Prior to arriving at my duty station, I was required to visit the Navy Space Fence in Dahlgren, Virginia, which also tracked space vehicles and was a part of the NORAD SPADATS system. The navy system projected beams of electrons into space; when a satellite passed through the fence, it was recorded in the control center.

The members of the team worked in shifts so that there would be coverage 24/7. We would work two midnight-to-seven shifts, two daytime shifts, and two swing shifts from four to midnight, and we would then have three days off. This was wonderful since in the winter we could go to the mountains and ski. (Back then, we could obtain a lift ticket for the entire family for $125 for the season, while today it cost close to $125 a day to ski.) My brother, Jess Maxwell, and I built a two-bedroom A-frame in Breckenridge, Colorado, where we spent many days skiing in the winter or fishing in the summer.

On one of the family ski outings, I was skiing down one of the medium slopes when a rather large man hit me from behind and we both went flying into the snow. As I was picking myself up, I tried to assist the other skier. However, he didn't want my help and said, "Why don't you go down to the beginner's slope where you belong?" Anyone who skis learns that the downhill skier always has the right-of-way, and in this case, I was the downhill skier. I told this very rude man that if he wanted to resolve this, I would meet him at the manager's office.

At the manager's office, he asked where I worked, and I told him NORAD in Colorado Springs. He then asked what my rank was, and when I told him I was a lieutenant, he pulled out his ID card, which stated "Colonel USAF," and said we would resolve this at the headquarters. I told him I was a lieutenant in the US Navy, which meant he could do nothing to me at work. Later, the navy captain I reported to found out what had happened and sent the good colonel a large, laminated ID card and a note that read, "For use on the ski slopes only." This did not make the colonel very happy.

While stationed in Colorado Springs, I flew the air force U3B, a twin-engine propeller Cessna 310, to stay proficient. Although the most dangerous flying I did was flying jets off aircraft carriers, I did almost crash in the U3B on a proficiency flight to El Paso, Texas. Descending in the clouds into El Paso, we flew into a small area of ice that completely covered my windscreen. I ordered the copilot to turn on the deicing, but since it was his first trip in the aircraft, he could not find the switch. I immediately declared an emergency and asked to be rerouted to Kirtland Air Force Base, the closest military facility. I was picked up by air traffic control and vectored to the base. Since Lackland had a twelve-thousand-foot runway, I felt I would have a better chance of landing safely. Once switched to a very professional air force approach controller, I was lined up and directed to a final landing. Though I still couldn't see anything out of my front cockpit window, I was able do fairly well looking out the side window. A very hard landing followed, but we were safely on the ground. In order for us to get to the terminal, the base personnel had to tow us to our parking spot. Of course, there were some jokes made when they found out the pilot was navy.

Two more memories stand out from my joint staff tour. The first is that, while I was on duty one midnight shift, the Russians launched their first satellite, *Sputnik 1*. This was a very exciting time, and everyone from the president down was very interested in what this event would mean. The on-duty officers in NORAD SPADATS were responsible for the briefing in the large air defense command control center. This very large room had ten radar stations on the floor of the center. Above the center was a large glassed-in area where all of the generals would sit at radar consoles. Our briefing position was a small perch halfway up the front wall above the noisy floor below. I later told my colonel that it was a good thing I had long pants on—I was so scared, my knees were knocking! One of the questions the four-star air force general asked was "Can the Soviets use their satellite to launch an atomic weapon?"

"We do not know," I said. "Much more technical research must be done before we can determine if the Soviets could use an earth satellite vehicle as a weapons platform." I was also proud to tell him that the first tracking of the satellite was done by the navy.

The other memorable event was that, after I was at the NORAD headquarters for two years, it was announced that President John F. Kennedy was going to visit the command center and was very interested in our space section since the launch of *Sputnik*. Since I was one of the longest-serving officers in SPADATS, I was chosen to be the briefing officer for the president's visit. I wrote a very thorough briefing and presented it to my boss, the air force colonel. He approved the briefing, and I was set to make the presentation. A week before the visit, we had a dress rehearsal in the command center. At the right time, I stepped out to the podium and gave my twenty-minute presentation. Following the briefing, the staff aide for the viewing general called my boss to tell him that although I had given an excellent presentation, he would prefer that an air force officer from his command give the briefing. After having worked so hard, I, of course, was very disappointed. The next day, I received a call from a colonel in the other command asking for a copy of my briefing. After checking with my boss, who was also upset about SPADATS not giving the briefing, he gave me permission to tell him that he would have to write his own brief. The colonel was very upset, and I am told he did not do a good job briefing the president because he knew very little about our work.

After being in Colorado for about two and a half years, I was asked where I would like to go for my upcoming sea duty tour. I had always wanted to fly jets, so I asked to be transferred to Whidbey Island, Washington, to fly the A3D Skywarrior. The Skywarrior, a twin-engine jet, was a carrier-based nuclear attack bomber similar to the one my grandson Trent visited on board the *Yorktown* in Charleston Harbor. The A3 was the largest jet to operate off navy carriers. I was very excited when I received orders to Heavy Attack Squadron Four in Oak Harbor, Washington.

CHAPTER 7

Returning to Sea Duty and Combat in Vietnam

Driving across Deception Pass toward Oak Harbor, my family and I were impressed with the natural beauty of Whidbey Island. As we approached Oak Harbor, I saw my first A3s flying over us. I had to get out of the car and watch them take off and land at the naval air station. Needless to say, this pilot was very excited to know that I would be flying the beautiful Skywarrior soon. It was my confirmation that I had chosen the right assignment.

However, Betty was not so sure and told me that I had brought her, Matt, and Debra "to the end of the earth" and that she was not too sure about me flying that large of an aircraft off navy carriers. We stayed in a motel with an indoor pool while looking for a place to rent, which made Matt and Debra very happy.

I immediately started intensive ground school, spending the next six months learning to fly the A3 Skywarrior. Above all other things, I was very concerned about flying an aircraft with a nuclear weapon on board. During training, we learned to navigate over low-level routes so we could proceed into enemy territory without being detected and loft a nuclear weapon onto a designated target. The flying was the most demanding I had ever done. Toward the end of my training, I completed my required twelve-day and six-night landings on board the USS *Independence* flying out of NAS Miramar Naval Air Station in Southern California. This was the final stage of the training, and I was now qualified to be a carrier-based single integrated operational plan (SIOP) pilot capable of delivering a nuclear weapon onto an enemy target.

During the training, we were also required to attend a one-week survival school with nothing to eat but bugs, fish, and snakes. At the end, we were captured by the enemy as prisoners of war and not treated very well for two or more days. When Betty, Matt, and Debra came to pick me up, I looked so bad they did not recognize me.

I received one week of leave after completing training and then reported to Heavy Attack Squadron Four (VAH-4) at Whidbey. Once in Heavy Four, I was assigned to Detachment Golf, which was one of the six detachments belonging to VAH-4. It was made up of three heavy attack Skywarriors, six pilots, six navigators, and sixty-five enlisted men, of whom six were trained as enlisted crewman navigators.

Detachment Golf was assigned to the USS *Oriskany*, a 27 Charlie small deck carrier. We started our workups for our deployment to the war in Vietnam in the early part of 1966. One of the more difficult tasks in flying the aircraft was inflight refueling. This was when the pilot would fly up behind the tanker and place his probe into the basket of the tanker. We were not taught this in the training squadron. At one point during the workup, we were required to escort four other A3s from Whidbey Island to Hawaii, a trip of about three thousand miles. I was at thirty-five thousand feet with four other A3s, and I had never refueled in flight before. If I failed to connect, the A3s would have to return to Whidbey, which would not have been good. With my command officer on my wing, I very nervously tried to connect to the tanker. After fifteen minutes, I finally was able to connect. We were only five minutes from having to turn around and return to Whidbey.

The remainder of the workup went well, and we completed several conventional bombing flights, which would be our primary mission in Vietnam. We deployed in early 1966, and after five days, we were off the coast of Oahu, Hawaii. Before we were allowed to join the Seventh Fleet, we had to pass our operational readiness inspection (ORI). Part of that inspection required us to have graded bombing practice and fly a real atomic bomb off the ship and land at Barbers Point Naval Air

Station. We actually were required to go through the drop procedure we would use if we ever had to use the weapon. The pilot had half of the drop code, and the bombardier navigator had the other half, so one crewmember could not drop the weapon on his own. The entire crew was relieved when we landed at Barbers Point and were taxied to a remote part of the field, where we were met by at least twenty marines with automatic weapons to protect what we were carrying. We passed our ORI with flying colors and were headed for the Gulf of Tonkin and the war in Vietnam.

In addition to being a heavy bomber, the A3 was configured as an airborne tanker, a gas station in the sky. When we arrived on station in Vietnam, it was decided that due to the size of the A3, its value as a tanker, and the sophistication of the new Russian SA2 ground-to-air missiles, the A3 would not be allowed to fly over the beach in North Vietnam.

During our first line period of four weeks, we conducted many tanking missions and some conventional bombing missions in South Vietnam, working with the army and dropping five-hundred-pound bombs. During the six months on the line, the detachment saved some thirty-five aircraft from going in the water. These aircraft had been hit in the wing during a bombing mission and were losing fuel too quickly to make it back to the ship without inflight refueling. We would meet them off the beach, they would plug in, and we would pump fuel to the aircraft until we reached the carrier. Then, they would disconnect and immediately land, sometimes with less than five minutes of fuel on board.

Not all missions had such positive endings, though. Tragedy came in October, just after the Oriskany made a visit to Hong Kong. We were operating with three carriers in the gulf, flying major strikes against the North from all three carriers. The tanker's mission was to launch at daybreak and find fighter and attack aircraft that needed fuel, pass on as much fuel as we could give away, and land on any of the three carriers to hot refuel (i.e., refuel with engines running) and catapult off to again pass fuel to the fighter and attack aircraft. There were days when we would not return to the *Oriskany* until sunset. After two days of flying this mission, I was totally exhausted, and at 7:00 p.m. on the October 25, I dropped in my bunk for a long overdue night's rest. I was not scheduled to fly until noon the next day, but at 10:00 p.m. my phone rang. The duty officer said the schedule had been changed, and I was now schedule for a 7:00 a.m. launch. Although I protested, it did no good.

I was up at 5:00 a.m. for a cold shower, an intelligence briefing at six, and man-up at six thirty. As I was sitting on the flight deck with engines running, ready for launch at seven, the forward starboard (right) side of the *Oriskany* exploded. Due to bad weather the evening before, all of the night flights had been cancelled. This required that all of the magnesium flares be removed from the strike aircraft and returned to the flare storage locker. As one of the flares was being placed in storage, it ignited. This caused the locker to violently explode, resulting in a massive fire. Six hours later, on October 26, 1966 (your grandmother's birthday), the fire was out. Forty-three crewmen had lost their lives, including two officers from our detachment: our officer in charge, Cdr. George Farris, and our operations officer, Lt. Cdr. Jim Smith. I had taken the flight originally assigned to Jim Smith, and my stateroom was destroyed in the fire. LTJG "Sig" Signorelli was in the ship's hospital, and I was now the senior officer of the detachment. Sig had been pulled off a body pile when a sailor heard him cough, gave him mouth-to-mouth, and saved his life. I don't know how long he was unconscious, but when I arrived in sickbay to check on him, he did not know who I was.

I immediately became the acting officer in charge responsible for the remaining men in our detachment. At that time, I was very unsure how to proceed with the responsibility of notifying the families of our fallen officers. I was blessed to have an exceptional Personnel Man Second class, Ralph Estes, who provided the administrative assistance I needed. At his encouragement, I gathered our detachment in the hangar bay to pay tribute to our lost and make sure the rest of the men were okay.

Following this meeting, I went to a dark and wet ready room to determine the damage to our flight records and flight gear. While there I was totally overcome with emotion for what had taken place. Not knowing what else to do, I dropped to my knees and, in a flood of tears, once again thanked a God I did not know personally for sparing my life.

Due to the disruption of communications, it would be three long days before your grandmother would know if I was alive. Also, having been thrust into a leadership role as the senior wife, Betty spent hours consoling the families of Jim Smith and George Farris. The wife of the Heavy Four commanding officer knew where my stateroom was and was very frightened that they had not gotten to my body to report the loss, so she remained very close to your grandmother. Not knowing what was known at home, we sent a wrap up message to the squadron on the third day after the fire. I signed the message "Lt. Commander Tom Maxwell, Acting Officer in Charge, sends." The commanding officer's wife went to our home very late that night and embraced your grandmother with this wonderful news.

The ship was destroyed beyond repair, and the *Oriskany* sailed home in early November. We offloaded two of the Skywarriors in the Philippines and flew home to Whidbey Island, arriving home to thankful families, but with very heavy hearts for our lost shipmates and their families. We had one month's rest and time with our families before we started our workup for our 1967 cruise on board the repaired *Oriskany*. Facing another six-month cruise was not easy, but that was what we'd signed on for.

Other than combat operations in the Gulf of Tonkin, several other things were eventful. In September, the East Coast carrier *Forestall* joined us in the gulf. Just as with the *Oriskany,* the *Forestall* sustained massive damage that required a return to the States. On July 26, during the ship's first combat launch, a zuni rocket went off and hit the plane that then Lt. Cdr. John McCain, later Senator McCain, was in. He escaped, but the ship was destroyed beyond repair. The *Forestall* headed home, and the trained pilots and crew were given the opportunity of transferring to our ship to fly combat missions. This was a very courageous step for the *Forestall* pilots, considering we had lost thirty-five flight crewmembers since arriving in the combat zone.

Lt. Cdr. John McCain was one of the *Forestall* pilots who volunteered to join *Oriskany*. On several flights, I refueled John's aircraft using our gas station in the sky. I was also in the air on October 26, your grandmother's birthday and one year after the *Oriskany* fire, when I heard "mayday, mayday, mayday!" from an A4 Skyhawk over Hanoi. It was Lt. Cdr. John McCain's aircraft. He'd landed in a lake with two broken legs and one broken arm. He then spent five years as a prisoner of war in Hanoi, the capital of North Vietnam. We called the Hanoi prison the "Hanoi Hilton." John's dad was a four-star admiral in charge of Vietnam operations. We were told that it was most difficult for his dad to order bombing raids on Hanoi knowing his son was being held captive there. Trying to obtain favor from Admiral McCain, the North Vietnamese offered John early release, which John refused since there were other POWs who had been held longer. This was a remarkable decision due to the treatment POWs were receiving.

One way the KA3 that we were flying had been successful was in saving combat jets that were coming off the beach with too little gas to return to the carrier. It was either receive gas from "Texaco" (our airborne gas station) or eject into the gulf. During the 1966 cruise, even with the fire, Detachment Golf had thirty-five saved aircraft. During the 1967 cruise, we had over fifty saves. One very special save is quoted as follows by the pilot involved: "Rescue efforts to recover downed Navy pilot Lt. Roger Duthie just southeast of Hanoi in the words of the F8 Crusader pilot, Lt. Commander Dick Shaffert, involved in the rescue effort.

"*Oriskany* had launched the KA-3s to top off the alpha strike and was trying to hot-spin (land/refuel/launch) one KA-3 to get some fuel back in the air, but all that was airborne was one A-4 buddy tanker to cover the recovery. Rules were that the tanker had to stay around the carrier traffic pattern while the ship was conducting air operations. God was in two cockpits that day! I felt his hands on the stick many times! He also inspired a hell of an A-4 driver by the name of Mac Davis to lie about his fuel state, take the fuel from the buddy tanker, and come on back in to help me!

When I heard Mac coming in, I knew we had a great chance to get Duthie if I could show him the position. So I changed my bingo calculations from making it back to the *Oriskany* to just making feet wet, where I could safely eject. Davis made a perfect rendezvous, and I dropped him off over Duthie as the Sandy's (rescue strike aircraft) reported 20 kilometers to the southwest. I was down to five hundred pounds and didn't really think I would make the water.

I was trying to give *Red Crown* (a USN destroyer) my likely ejection position when Tom Maxwell came up on the frequency. His KA-3 detachment had dozens of saves (fuel to return to the ship) during that cruise, and I got two of them in the first two weeks on the line! It was against all the rules for those guys to go feet dry in the area for known SAM (surface-to-air missile) firings, but Tom gave me the same break I had given Duthie and came on in. He swung in front of me with his drogue extended and the APR-27 (missile warning device) blaring in our ears. After plug-in, I glanced down at the gauge and saw it rising past the first index mark from zero. When I disconnected with 2,500 pounds, the Jolly Green (rescue helicopter) reported the successful pickup of Duthie".

When the emergency call from Dick was broadcast, I realized that, as pilot, I could make the decision to go in harm's way and break the commander's rules about KA3 aircraft over the beach. However, I also knew that I was responsible for the lives of two other crewmen: Lt. Jim VanderHoek and Petty Officer First Class Bill Shelton. Understanding that responsibility, I turned to look at each crewman, and without a word, I got a thumbs-up from both. Jim immediately turned to the task of preparing the refueling system and P.O. Shelton to monitoring our radar warning equipment.

Back on board the *Oriskany* and during our debriefing, we admitted to breaking the rules to our officer in charge, Cdr. Bill Laurentis. We all agreed that there were times in war when action to save a life is required and that sometimes we will need to go into harm's way. There was truly no time to get permission to save the life of a valuable navy fighter and a superb fighter pilot. It is also very meaningful that your grandfather remains in contact with the pilot, Dick Shaffert, and he often reminds me of July 18, 1967. Recently, when Dick found out that I was involved in prison ministry, he said to me, "It looks as if you are still in the business of saving lives."

One other interesting mission took place in November 1967. I had been involved in two major strike efforts during an afternoon mission. On my return to *Oriskany* I was taxied over to the ship's island and told I was going to be hot-refueled (engines running) and was going to fly a passenger to Tan Son Nhut Air Force base in Saigon. My bombardier navigator (BN) was instructed to depart the airplane—my new passenger would ride in the BN's seat. I asked over the air who my passenger would be. I was told that the skipper of VF-162, Cdr. Dick Bellinger, had just shot down the first Russian-built MiG-21 with an F8 Crusader in the Vietnam War and that I was taking him to Saigon for a national press briefing.

Some time passed until the commander climbed the ladder and jumped into the BN seat. Our Crewman Navigator helped him get his headset plugged in so we could communicate. The flight deck was very anxious to taxi us out to the catapult since we were holding up the recovery. I asked Commander Bellinger if he was going to put on his seatbelt.

"Are you going to crash?" he asked.

"No sir," I said.

Then he said "Let's launch!"

This was certainly not safe. It was clear at this point that the flight surgeon had given the commander some medicinal brandy. Once airborne, I needed to file a new flight plan to Saigon, and I was sure I was not going to get any help from my new crewman. I tried to entertain the commander by asking him about his shoot down. That worked for a while—until he said, "Tom, I have never flown an A3." I thought to myself, *and you are not going to fly one today.*

My compromise with the commander was that I would execute a victory roll over the air force base in Saigon before landing. Descent and approach went well, and I asked the tower for a flyover and a break to downwind for landing. Over the field, at 1,500 feet, I pulled the nose up, rolled the aircraft 360 degrees, broke left, and landed.

Immediately after landing, I saw a blue air force jeep with a flag following the aircraft. Once we were clear of the runway, the tower asked us to stop and open our hatch so the air force colonel in the jeep could join us in the cockpit. I turned to the commander and said, "Sir, he is all yours." Commander Bellinger climbed down the ladder and proceeded to tell the colonel who he was and what he had done. He then got a hero's ride to base operations with the colonel. I taxied in and refueled to be prepared to return to the *Oriskany*. In base operations was a message telling us to return to the ship ASAP with Commander Bellinger. He insisted we attend his press conference, which we did.

Needless to say, he was a rather flamboyant fighter pilot, with the nick name of "Belly One", and he had much to say about the shoot down. Following the briefing, we headed to base operations to file for our return to the carrier. The commander was not going to join us but instead said he deserved at least a couple of nights to celebrate. Two days later, our boss, Commander Laurentis, was required to return to Saigon to bring home the now famous skipper.

Shortly after this, we found out that we were going to Hong Kong for Christmas. Two other officers and I were selected to fly there early to arrange for a ship Christmas party at the Hong Kong Hilton. After all the work was done with the ship due in the next morning, which was Christmas Eve, your foolish grandfather rented the Hilton's three-mast schooner to go out and meet the *Oriskany* as she sailed into the Hong Kong harbor. So at six in the morning, we sailed out to meet the carrier, circling her as she sailed in. When my boss saw us on the sailing ship, he could not believe it. I also got in real trouble with your grandmother since I charged the ship on her American Express card. When I called her on Christmas day, she told me that it was fine—except Matt and Debra would not eat for a week.

Another prank that almost got us in trouble was when returning to the Oriskany very late the night before the ship sailed, we ran into a Chinese man selling live chickens. Several of us from the detachment purchased a rooster, placed him in a sack and then returned him to the ship, hoping he would not crow as we crossed the quarter deck, where you receive permission to board. Once safely on board we took him to the stateroom of our dearly beloved flight surgeon and let him loose and closed the door. None of us could understand why we heard nothing from the flight surgeon about his guest visitor. That is until we pulled into our next port of call in the Philippines. The night before steaming into Subic Bay, when they normally announce when the ship's crew will have shore leave, the ship's Captain came on the ship's all hands announcement system. He said, "unfortunately there will be no shore leave for the crew in Subic since the ship is under a medical quarantine. He said that someone brought a live chicken on board the ship in Hong Kong that was infected with a disease that could be communicated to humans". The three officers, including your grandfather, panicked since we were sure we were going to be in serious trouble. The culprits were allowed to stew for over two hours. As the crew got more upset, our favorite flight surgeon showed up at the ready room announcing, "who is going to get the last laugh"? It was only then that we learned that he had talked the captain into making the announcement. He also told us he got up the next morning with chicken do do all over his stateroom. I know he knew what squadron had done the deed but not sure he knew your grandfather was involved.

After one more line period in the gulf, we headed home in February 1968. At the end of the line period, I had flown two hundred combat missions and could not fly any more. We flew home from the Philippines with three A3s, stopping at Okinawa, Wake Island, and Hawaii, about a seven-thousand-mile journey.

The Reflections of a Naval Pilot Going To His First Overseas Shore Assignment—Rota, Spain—and Flying an EA3B Spy Aircraft against the Soviet Union during the Cold War

After I'd spent some time at home in Whidbey, we departed for our new assignment in Rota, Spain. Your grandfather, your grandmother, Matt, and Debra headed east to New York City with a stop in Boonville to visit the town and your grandmother's parents. Prior to leaving Oak Harbor, I was able to book passage on the USS *United States* from New York to Bremerhaven in Northern Germany. I also ordered a new Volkswagen Beetle to be delivered in Bremerhaven on our arrival.

We stopped in Washington, DC, so we could pick up our tickets and stateroom assignment. The lady in charge said we were very fortunate: Lieutenant Commander Maxwell was the senior naval officer on the trip, so we would have first class accommodations. Wow, was that great—until we found out we would have to dress formal each night for dinner. So I headed for the store to buy formal attire for the trip.

As we left Washington, I hurt my back, so Betty, Matt, and Debra had to carry all of the bags when we arrived at the ship. I know everyone who watched us thought badly of this big man having his family carry all the bags. It was a wonderful five days at sea with great food and accommodations. The famous painter Salvador Dalí was on board with us and got much attention. Matt and Debra found out how to sneak down to the second-class spaces, which they said were more fun.

When we arrived in Germany, I picked up our new car, which was very small. How we got two adults, two children, and eight bags into that car I will never know. Much of the luggage was on a rack on top of the car. We truly did look like Wally World as we started the five-day drive south to Rota, Spain. The trip was fun but a bit stressful since we spoke no German, French, or Spanish. We attempted to stay at military facilities where English was spoken until we entered France, where we had to stop at a new motel where the only language was French, the menu included. The staff was very kind to us and helped us order our meals. Matt and Debra were not very happy with our salami-and-cheese breakfast. When we paid, I gave the employees a new one-dollar bill, which they proudly put up on the wall.

Our next stop was Barcelona, Spain, where we had dinner at a snail restaurant. Debra tried to make her brother sick, eating every one of her snails and telling Matt, who was ready to throw up, how wonderful they were. We stopped in Madrid, the capital of Spain, before arriving at the naval air station in Rota. Since there were no quarters available on base, we had to rent a Spanish home until we could get base housing. Needless to say, it was a real experience living among Spanish people when we spoke no Spanish. It was only a few months before we received housing, the back of our house looking out over the Mediterranean Sea. We also had a wonderful Spanish maid who came every day to help Betty. As I was getting settled into the squadron, Betty was becoming a tourist, learning to watch bullfights and golfing weekly with the ladies.

After a short time learning about the secret mission of the EA3B, I was called into the operation officer's office and told that I was going to Danang, Vietnam, to help the other VQ squadron flying combat missions against the North Vietnamese.

"Sir," I said, "I have already completed two hundred combat missions, and the navy said that is all you should fly."

"Great!" he replied. "That is just the kind of experience we need so go pack your bags."

All I could say was "Yes, sir!"

Betty was not very happy, since I had just returned from a six-month cruise. Two months and fifty combat missions later, I returned to Spain and VQ-2.

Trent, if you remember the EA3B we visited on the flight deck of the USS *Yorktown* in Charleston Harbor in 2011, that was the aircraft I flew in Vietnam. Someday you can show your children the aircraft your grandfather flew fifty combat missions in.

Back in Rota, I was assigned numerous short deployments to England, Norway, Germany, Italy, and Greece, as well as aboard numerous aircraft carriers, all flying and collecting intelligence against the Soviet Union. On one detachment to Bodo, Norway, we were flying against the Soviet's North Sea exercises. It was our job to collect electronics and communications intelligence in order to help the United States understand the capabilities of the Soviet fleet.

On one such flight, I was shadowing a Soviet Badger, and he spotted me and attempted to outrun me. I pulled up behind him, and the gunner in the rear held up a bottle of American beer and then aimed his guns at our aircraft. As we broke off, we were just south of Iceland, and I realized that, because I had chased the Badger, I did not have enough fuel to make it back to Norway. My only choice was to call and see if we could land and refuel at Lossiemouth, Scotland. Since I had not filed a flight plan to Scotland, the British scrambled fighters to intercept us and escorted our aircraft to the airfield. We arrived at midnight, and the duty officer was not very happy with us, since he'd had to send out the fighters to identify us. As we flew back to Bodo, it started to get light. It was summer, and the entire time we were in Norway the sun never set—it was daytime during our entire two weeks there. I was thankful that the windows in our hotel had black shades so that we could sleep. Many tourists fly up to Bodo in the summer just to see the beautiful sun sink in the west, touch the horizon, and then climb back into the sky without ever setting.

During many missions, we collected electronic and communications intelligence against the Russians. Two additional missions that were other than routine were flown off the carrier USS Independence and out of Ramstein Air Force Base in Germany. Once a month, we would deploy there for three days and fly missions in the Baltic off the coast of the Soviet Union. At sunrise, we would taxi out to the end of the runway and would have absolutely no communications with the control tower, so no one would know we were departing. At the end of the runway, we would taxi past all the waiting air force aircraft and wait for the green light from the tower that cleared us for takeoff. Once airborne, we held strict radio silence with air traffic control until our return to Ramstein. For the four-hour mission, we would monitor a special intelligence radio, listening for the code that would recall us if they felt we were in danger. Gary Powers was shot down in his U-2 spy aircraft on May 1, 1960, with an SA-2 missile in this area of the Soviet Union.

Once we crossed the shoreline into the Baltic, we would head for the Soviet coast, remaining outside the three-mile limit of their airspace.

If we flew into their airspace, they were authorized to shoot us down. Due to the secret nature of the mission, we would often go undetected; however, every so often the Russians would scramble Mig fighters to intercept our aircraft and fake a shoot down. After closing on us, they would light up our collection equipment with their fire-control radar, which meant they were locked on our aircraft and with one pull of their missile trigger they would blow us out of the sky. The backseat operator would always put the fire control warble on the A3s intercommunications system so that the entire crew could hear it in their headset.

Only once during these flights did we receive an emergency recall, and it was during an event like those described above. We turned immediately west, added power, and dove for the deck (water). We could only assume that our intelligence folks had intercepted a communications giving the fighter permission to fire. Having used more fuel than planned, we neared Ramstein with low fuel and bad weather conditions. As we approached we were told that the field was below minimums, which meant we could not land. When the air traffic controller asked what our divert field was, I told him we had none since we did not have enough fuel to reach our divert field. We were then turned over to a Ramstein ground control approach (GCA), and the controller talked us, against his rules, through a safe landing. We did not see the runway until almost touchdown. If it had not been for an extremely good air control operator, we may have had no choice but to bail out. The squadron sent an official message to the GCA unit commending them for their professionalism, given that they had saved an aircraft and crew. As we sipped an adult beverage at the officers' club that evening, we listened to the air force pilots complaining about this navy aircraft with no markings always getting to go to the head of the line. We just smiled with no comment.

The second collection mission that I remember as being memorable was when I was assigned to take a one-plane detachment onto the carrier USS *Independence*, which was steaming just south of Italy. We had been on board for about a week, flying collection missions against Soviet ships in the Mediterranean Sea with some excellent results.

Late one evening, the ship operations officer called me and said that I was to report to the admiral's chief of staff to discuss a special mission. I found out that the Soviets had sailed their first aircraft carrier, a helicopter and vertical landing aircraft carrier named *Moskva*, out of the Black Sea and into the Mediterranean Sea. I had the only aircraft on board the carrier that carried enough fuel to reach the *Moskva* and return to the *Independence*. I briefed the admiral that the EA3B carried great electronic intelligence collection capability, but our only photographic equipment was a handheld camera. I also advised him that we were restricted to not flying closer than five hundred feet over Russian ships. I vividly remember him saying, "Commander, I want pictures, so do what you have to get them." My answer was, of course, "Aye, aye, sir."

We spent a large part of the evening researching the electronics on the *Moskva*, and the crew became very excited when they learned the ship had the first Soviet ship three-dimensional radar in the world and that we had a shot at collecting the very first intelligence on the radar.

The following morning, we briefed, loaded, and launched for the *Moskva*. We were some two hundred miles from the ship when we picked up the first emissions that were unique to the *Moskva*, so we had little trouble finding her. On the inbound leg, the ELINT crew in the back was ecstatic with what they were collecting. Once we sighted the ship, we dropped down for our photo run, and I made two passes up the starboard and port sides of the ship, remembering my instructions from the admiral, at one hundred feet. The right seat operator told me we had obtained some excellent shots.

As we pulled up to depart, the crew asked if I was going to welcome the *Moskva* to the carrier navy by making a carrier approach to the ship. So I returned and did something I knew I should not have done. I flew up the starboard side of the carrier, broke left, and on the downwind leg, lowered my flaps, landing gear, and tail hook like I was going to land. We all knew we could not land on a helicopter carrier, but as we approached the ship, so many red flares went off it became like the Fourth of July. We immediately cleaned up and returned to the *Independence* with just enough fuel to make the return trip. We were nothing short of heroes when the ship started processing both our electronic and photo intelligence. The chief of staff called to say the admiral was very pleased with our collection mission.

What none of us knew at the time was that a US Navy destroyer that we had seen was shadowing the *Moskva* and that there was a surface (a ship driver, not an aviator) admiral on board. This admiral sent a flash message (for use in wartime only) to the navy staff in Washington, DC, saying that an unmarked navy A3 had flown through the *Moskva* traffic pattern at fifty feet or less during flight operations. Needless to say, I got to revisit the admiral, who asked, "Did you really have to fly that low?"

I answered, "Sir, you instructed me to do what I needed to do to get productive pictures."

He had great integrity and professionally protected me from getting in serious trouble. I was very fortunate that the destroyer admiral did not mention our making a carrier-landing pass.

Also, after looking at the intelligence we collected, my commanding officer privately commended the entire crew. There were thirteen frequencies on the new 3-D radar, and we had documented eleven of them, pleasing the intelligence community greatly. Shortly after this event, I was selected to return to the Navy Postgraduate School in Monterey, California, to study aeronautical engineering. My family and I were very pleased to return home.

CHAPTER 8

Shore Duty and Squadron Command Selection

Your grandfather was going back to school at an older age and had chosen to get his master's degree in aeronautical engineering. I was also the senior officer in the class, so I had additional duties leading all the officers in my class. There was one thing I was dead sure of: I was not going to turn out for six-man tackle football again! Since I'd been out of school for many years, the curriculum was very difficult, and I cannot tell you how many hours I spent studying for the many very technical subjects I was taking.

This time we did not live in navy housing, residing instead in Pacific Grove, right next to Monterey, California. Our house was just a block from a beautiful beach, so in the evening, we often walked there. Some very memorable things happened while we were there. The most important was that we found out that Grandmother was pregnant with your dad, Mike. We had only planned to have Matt and Debra, so though surprised, we were excited to have another son, your special dad.

After we had been at Monterey for about a year, I was selected to be promoted to commander (lieutenant colonel). After such promotions, the navy would screen the officers to select commanding officers of naval aircraft squadrons. During the screening, I was selected to be the commanding officer (CO) of Tactical Electronic Warfare Squadron 135 (VAQ-135) at Naval Air Station Alameda in California. I would report to the squadron as the executive officer

(XO) for a year, and then, at a change-of-command ceremony, I would take command of the squadron. I had a very difficult decision to make. If I stayed at the postgraduate school and finished my master's degree, I would lose my selection to become a CO. Since the goal of every naval aviator is to command his own squadron, I chose to take a Bachelor of Science degree in aeronautical engineering, move my family to Alameda, and become the XO of VAQ-135, the world-famous Black Ravens.

Reflections of Returning to Operational Flying in a Senior Leadership Position

I reported to VAQ-135 at Alameda Naval Air Station in October 1971. One of the most important things that happened while we were in Alameda was that on January 15, 1972, your dad was born at Oak Knoll Naval Hospital in Oakland, California. We lived on Alameda Island, about twenty minutes from the naval air station.

The VAQ-135 Black Ravens were flying the EKA3D Skywarrior, which was configured both as an airborne tanker—a gas station in the sky—and as an electronic jammer. The entire squadron did not deploy on board a single carrier but sent three plane detachments to be a part of the navy air wing, similar to the way we had deployed in Heavy Attack Squadron four. We had three detachments, and one was deployed on board the USS *Hancock* when I arrived.

Shortly after I arrived, we received a request from the USS *Hancock* detachment for a new A3, as they had broken one of theirs. Since I was new and needed to know more about how VAQ-135 operated at sea, I volunteered to fly the new A3 out to Cubi Point Naval Air Station in the Philippine Islands. It is a trip of over seven thousand miles, and we landed in Hawaii, on Wake Island, on Guam, and finally at Cubi Point. The *Hancock* had sent a pilot and crew to return the aircraft back on board the ship. Since I was not current in my carrier qualifications, I had to fly on board *Hancock* sitting in the fourth seat on the floor of the cockpit. I did not like this seat at all, since I could see nothing but sky. A week later, after observing flight operations, with another A3, we returned to Alameda, having been gone for just over a month.

As we taxied up to the VAQ-135 hangar doors and shut down the engines, the hangar doors started to open, and there was a large "Welcome Home VAQ-135 Detachment 0" sign and lots of folks to meet us. There was a band made up of some of the children from the squadron with a sign reading "Scrunch Bird"—they were not that good. There was, of course, your grandmother, your uncle, your aunt, and your dad in a stroller. When I went over to cut the welcome-home cake with a navy sword, I found out it was a "box cake"—the maintenance officer, Pat Walsh, had put icing on a cardboard box as a joke.

We enjoyed our time in Alameda. Matt and Debra, who were in middle school, enjoyed taking care of your dad, who was a handful. We lived just across the street from a canal, and when they were not racing him around the block in his stroller, Matt and Debra would take Michael there to watch the ships going through the canal.

After about a year, I took command of VAQ-135 at a change-of-command ceremony. This time we had a real cake and a real band. We had someone babysit your dad in the CO's office so he would not interrupt the ceremony. This was what Grandpa had worked for during his twenty years in the navy, and it was his next professional step up the promotional ladder.

Shortly after taking command of the squadron, I received a call from the Bureau of Naval Personnel informing me that VAQ-135 had been selected to move north to NAS Whidbey Island in Washington and transition into the new EA-6B Prowler. I was asked how I felt about taking on this task. We were all very excited, since it would mean that I would be CO for two years instead of one, fly a new jet, and move back to a place we all loved. So we transferred our remaining detachments to VAQ-130, packed up our squadron, gathered our household goods, and moved north, finding a chief petty officer to drive our loudly painted squadron car to Whidbey.

Reflections on Our Transition to the EA-6B Prowler in VAQ-129 in September 1973 and the Commissioning of the VAQ-135 Black Ravens as an EA-6B Squadron in January 1975

When we arrived on Whidbey Island, we were assigned base housing that had a beautiful view of the Puget Sound. Your grandpa started transition training, and Uncle Matt and Aunt Debra went back to middle school. Shortly after moving in, we had the opportunity to buy a lot and build our first home. The lot was off Swantown Road and was beautifully wooded. It was very exciting to actually own our home and make changes that fit our family. It was a four-bedroom, three-bath house, so we all had our own bedrooms, including Michael, who started preschool there. In addition to the bedrooms, we had a loft bed behind the kitchen that Michael would sneak into to sleep.

That small room was also where our cats were born. One morning, three kittens were under Grandpa's car in the driveway. I did not see them, and when I backed out, I ran over the cats. Betty, Matt, and Debra were very upset, and I was called all kinds of bad names! When everyone realized that there was no way for me to have known about the cats, they apologized and promised not to mention it again. However, when Grandpa came home, the kitten that had survived was named "Lucky."

While the squadron was in training, our family faced one of the most difficult medical crises that your grandparents had experienced. During a routine physical examination, the doctors found a spot on the upper left lobe of Betty's lung. A quick trip to Madigan Army Hospital at Fort Lewis, Washington, confirmed that it was a tumor, and the doctor recommended immediate surgery to remove it. In 1974, this was an extremely difficult and dangerous operation. As we left the hospital, stopping at the ferry landing prior to crossing to Whidbey Island, I remember being very frightened. It was at this same landing many years later that your grandfather would find the roots of his faith. Unfortunately, as I sat there the first time, what I would offer in prayer to the Lord was once again mechanical, since I had not asked the Lord into my life—even though years earlier in Hawaii the Lord had saved your uncle Matt through prayer.

I immediately decided to fly your grandmother Betty back to Barns Hospital in St. Louis, where she had trained as a registered nurse and where I knew she would receive better care than at an army hospital. In the process of making arrangements to return to St. Louis, I called a dear friend I had gone to Kemper Military School with, Dr. Herb Kaufman. Herb asked me to give him a day to research the possibility of thoracic surgery for Betty, whom he had known when Betty and I were dating at Kemper—long before we were married. Herb called the following day to tell me to not change our plans, since Betty's doctor at Fort Lewis was the best thoracic surgeon on the West Coast. Herb then gave me a gift that I did not deserve nor expect. He said, "Tom, I will cancel all of my appointments and fly up to Seattle to be with you during the surgery."

Days later, Betty and I made our way to the Madigan hospital. On the day of surgery, I was checking to make sure she was okay and ready when she told me she was not. When the doctor made his rounds before surgery, Betty told him she had changed her mind, remembering a thoracic surgery she'd seen in nurses' school. The doctor, Betty, and I talked through her concerns. After resolving this dilemma, I left to go pick up Herb at the Seattle airport. We returned to the hospital in time to see her before they took her into surgery. I proceeded to nervously pace the floor for the next four hours.

Because Herb was a medical doctor, they let him enter the surgical suite. He returned with a smile to tell me that the doctor had said that the surgery had gone well, but that they'd had to remove the lobe where the tumor had been. Knowing that I could not see my wife for several hours, I took Herb back to the airport, telling him that I did not know how I could ever repay him. Herb was Jewish, and, after I found Christ, I shared my faith with him throughout our friendship. He passed away several years ago, and I can only pray I will see him in paradise. We are blessed to be in touch with his wonderful ex-wife Margret, who lives the San Francisco Bay Area.

When I returned to the hospital, the nurse told me that the doctor had been looking for me, and I became deeply troubled. When I was finally able to speak with him, he shared with me that even though the surgery itself had gone well, when Betty was moved to the intensive care unit, the doctors and nurses could not get her to wake up from the heavy anesthetic required for the surgery. He explained that because of the severe pain following this type of surgery, the body sometimes does not want to wake up and that it had taken over an hour of using radical procedures that the doctors and nurses were able to bring her out of a coma.

Several hours later, when I was permitted to be by her bedside, I could not believe how bad she looked. In the early morning, as I returned home, I was exhausted, and I must have slept for eight solid hours while Betty's mom took care of your dad, aunt, and uncle. I lost track of how many two-hour trips I made to Fort Lewis. Grandmother Dowling was a great help and remained with Matt, Debra, and Michael until Betty came home. Two lab reports that followed had two different results: one said the tumor was not cancerous, and the other indicated it could possibly be a low-grade cancer. We were all so thankful to have mom back, but we failed to thank the Lord for her healing. The members of the squadron were incredibly supportive, both during the crises and after their CO's wife came home. It was truly like having a large extended family.

As Betty improved, I was able to focus more on the training we were doing in my squadron. Things were going well, except that the squadron had to complete survival school while going through this transition. I was exempt since I had previously been through the seven days of not-so-fun training, but because I was the commanding officer, I thought I should go through the training with my men. This was huge mistake, since the senior officer always receives harsher treatment than the junior officers and the enlisted men. We reported on Monday morning and received nothing to eat for the entire week. All we ate was what we found in the wooded area or in the ocean. We had no fish hooks, so we had to make them out of wire. In four days, I ate one small fish and a snake.

On Thursday of that week, we were given a set course to sneak through while the enemy was looking for us. I was captured around noon. When my guard was not looking, I escaped, only to be recaptured in about a half hour. My escape only made things worse for me, since when they caught me the second time, my previous guard put my head in a mud puddle facedown with his boot on the back of my head. A rock in the puddle cut my head open, and when he finally let me up, I was bleeding. *Good,* I thought. *He is going to have to administer first aid.* But I had no such luck and had to take care of it with my t-shirt.

During the remaining very long hours, we were treated harshly, and I spent twelve hours in a box measuring about three feet by four feet. We were not allowed to sleep for the remaining two days, and the enemy guards interrogated us for hours on end. This all was to show us what would take place if we were captured. When Betty came to pick me up, like the last time, she did not even recognize me. She cried, and I finally broke down and cried with her. Needless to say, when I got home, Betty dumped me in a hot tub to soak, and I received much TLC from my family, along with a wonderful meal.

The rest of our training was uneventful, and we went to the carrier to complete our qualifications in December 1974 on board the USS *Ranger* out of San Diego, California. The squadron and crews were now ready to commission a new chapter for the world-famous Black Ravens, now flying EA-6Bs.

Grandpa enjoyed his tour as commanding officer. We had four EA-6B jammer aircraft, seventeen officers, and 145 enlisted men. Since many of us had been together since Alameda, we had become a very professional team, which showed when we deployed for workups on board the USS *Ranger*. In addition to the Black Raven car, VAQ-135 also had a mascot called the Golden Goddess, or GG. GG had been a heavy attack (A3D Skywarrior) trophy originally stolen from in front of Tim's Restaurant, an Alameda establishment, the night before the carrier USS *Independence* was to sail for a Pacific cruise. GG was a young lady about five feet tall and painted gold. She was present for Grandpa's stand-up ceremony and for my change of command a year later.

If all the stories about GG were told, they would fill another journal. However, I need to tell at least one of GG's many escapades.

When not displayed, GG was hidden in a secret place so as not to be stolen. However, prior to leaving Alameda, the squadron removed GG from hiding and scheduled a lunch at Tim's Restaurant to celebrate her return to her original home. The owner found the retired bartender who had been on duty the night of the heist, and he joined us for lunch. The former bartender retold the story of the rather inebriated chiefs who made off with GG. When the story was written up in the Alameda newspaper, one of our sister A3 reserve squadrons discovered where GG was located and, several nights later, raided our duty office and stole our beloved mascot. Since the reserve squadrons only worked on weekends, they lifted GG forty feet in the air in their entry stairwell and welded her bottom steel plate to a steel girder in clear view of all who entered.

Some very upset junior officers put in place the plan to recover her. During the week, the reserve squadron only had a duty officer, a petty officer assistant, and a small full-time maintenance crew working on their A3 aircraft. Several weeks later, two of our junior officers and one petty officer skilled in welding borrowed a naval air station utility vehicle and, clad in protective coveralls, showed up at the reserve squadron with spray canisters in hand. The head culprit went to the duty office on the second deck and informed the ensign duty officer that he was from the naval air station public works and that, since the squadron was not working, the base had selected their hangar to be sprayed down for insects. The ensign was told that all personnel needed to be evacuated until the following day. It took about an hour to clear the hangar and then the "insect" team went to work removing GG from the stairwell. It took almost two hours using a high-lift to unweld GG's base and remove her from the stairwell. Once freed, GG was returned to hiding and the duty officer was told he could return to work. The last we heard, there was a young ensign looking for a new assignment. This was certainly not GG's most spectacular exploit. Once, a young ensign jumped off the deck of an aircraft carrier in port in Japan while attempting to steal GG from the onboard A3 squadron. This was how the famous GG remained a mascot of the famous Black Ravens.

The Black Raven squadron car was always driven in the annual Oak Harbor Days parade. One year stands out in my memory. I was driving the car and Betty was in the front seat as we passed through town in the parade. About halfway through the parade route, we saw Michael standing on the curb, and when he saw us, he started to cry. You can guess what happened next. We stopped the entire parade while Betty got out and brought your dad to the car with a large smile on his face! Michael was happy, but we couldn't say the same for the parade marshals.

During my command, VAQ-135 also became the first navy squadron to join the Oak Harbor Chamber of Commerce. By joining, we were able to do a lot to support the city we lived in, like give the chamber building a new coat of paint and refurbish the flower garden.

As noted above, we were going through workups, preparing to deploy for six months to the Pacific. Due to my scheduling, my change of command (CofC) would come before the squadron deployed. Several months before my CofC, the operations officer on the USS *Ranger* asked me if I would consider taking the job as the *Ranger*'s air operations officer, with the possibility of then becoming the ship's operations officer. Since I would be leaving home for six months or more, we had many discussions as a family before we decided that in the best interest of Matt, Debra, and Michael, I should take the job. This would mean Matt and Debra could finish high school in Oak Harbor and not have to move again. Also, since the *Ranger* was scheduled to move to the Bremerton Naval Shipyard in Washington state following the cruise, the family would not have to move until I left the *Ranger*.

I completed my tour as commanding officer in October 1975. We had a wonderful change-of-command ceremony where your grandfather turned over command of his beloved Black Ravens to Cdr. Dick Gunderman. And yes, GG was present at the ceremony, with four of our largest sailors guarding her. Shortly after the ceremony, I said good-bye to my special family and reported to the USS *Ranger* at the North Island Naval Air Station in San Diego, California.

CHAPTER 9

Going to Sea in Ships and My Spiritual Challenge

One of the things I was going to enjoy was having my own stateroom and sharing a bathroom with only one other officer. I also was going to enjoy working with my old squadron, who would deploy with Air Wing 16 on board *Ranger*. Another great benefit was that each Friday a navy C-9 (like an airliner) would depart NAS North Island nonstop to NAS Whidbey Island in Oak Harbor and return to North Island on Sunday, so I could get free transportation home on the weekends. So before and after the cruise, when we were not at sea, I did get to see the family often.

The air operations officer (AirOps) is responsible for all the air operations (AirOps) of the embarked air wing when there is weather around the ship and at night, when the aircraft were flying by instrument flight rules (IFR) and not visual flight rules (VFR). I had an elevated chair in AirOps and a big communications panel where I would sit whenever the ship was operating under IFR conditions. In front of me were several large, clear plastic boards where my men would write backward everything that was going on around the ship in the air. I knew the call sign for every aircraft (Raven 611), the type aircraft (EA-6B), the pilot's name (Tom Maxwell), and how much fuel he had on board (two thousand pounds). I was the officer who, when a pilot was having a problem landing on board, would send him up to get more gas or "bingo" the pilot to a land-based runway (send him or her to the beach to land). I also had to my right the carrier-controlled approach (CCA) enlisted men who would talk the pilot down the flight path to an arrested landing. These highly trained radar operators worked under the watchful eye of a highly trained Chief Petty Officer (CPO) who had much experience as an air traffic controller. I was blessed to have some exceptional air controllers who were very professional and who saved the lives of many of the air wing pilots.

A fun thing happened just before we deployed to the Pacific. We had a group of training squadron pilots on the ship to get their carrier qualifications (CarQuals) before they reported to their operational squadron. Some of the EA-6B pilots from Whidbey, a sister squadron to my old squadron, were getting their qualifications. After one of the landings, they found that one of the EA-6Bs had a bad starboard engine. The aircraft was dropped by elevator to the hangar deck, where the maintenance men changed the engine. Rules state that following an engine change, only a qualified EA-6B test pilot could fly the test flight for the aircraft. I was the only qualified test pilot on board, so after getting permission from my boss, I suited up, and on November 26, 1975, I flew my last operational flight in a navy aircraft. The catapult shot was great, and the plan was that I would fly to NAS Miramar, north of San Diego, where the new executive officer of VAQ-130 would be waiting to take the airplane to Whidbey Island. Once airborne, I turned to my ECM/navigator and said, "Contact San Diego Air Traffic Control," and changed our flight plan from NAS Miramar to NAS Whidbey Island with a hot refueling stop at NAS Alameda. Since the crew was from Whidbey, they were delighted. Your grandmother was very happily waiting at Whidbey, but the XO was unhappily waiting at NAS Miramar, with no airplane to fly home. The flight was great, the stop at Alameda went smoothly, and all was fine until I taxed up to the VAQ-130 hangar at Whidbey and was met by the squadron CO, who also was not happy, since VAQ-130 had a party scheduled that evening to welcome the new XO. I said, "Sorry, but this is my payment for doing your squadron's work as test pilot." Grandmother,

Matt, Debra, and your dad were in the parking lot outside the hangar with big smiles. Yes, this was the one and only time grandfather stole a navy aircraft.

Trent, this was your grandfather's last operational Navy flight and after almost 20 years of operational flying I had completed a total of 4,722 hours and 670 carrier landings having flown the below Navy aircraft: T34B, T28, SNJ, P2V, JD (Air Force B-26), SNB, S2F, T2J, A3D, KA3D, EKA3D, EA3B and the EA6B. Fourteen different Navy aircraft, flying 250 combat missions in Vietnam in the A-3 Skywarrior in both the North and the South. Operational aircraft were: The S2F Tracker with a total of 580 hours with 134 day and 64 night carrier landings, the A3D Skywarrior with 2,138 hours with 325 day and 82 night carrier landings and the EA6B Prowler with 373 hours with 58 day and 7 night carrier landings. First flight was in a T34B on April 27th 1956 and last in an EA6B on Nov 26th 1975.

Shortly after Christmas, I returned to San Diego to prepare for our six-month cruise to the Pacific. Early one morning in January 1976, we departed North Island and sailed out into the Pacific to prepare to recover all the aircraft that would ride *Ranger* for the next six months. Once the recovery was complete, we headed west for our first stop in Pearl Harbor, Hawaii. Prior to going into port, we embarked the inspection team from the staff of the commander of the Pacific Fleet. These men would conduct the *Ranger*'s operational readiness inspection. Every war-fighting capability of the ship would be tested, including air operations. We were all very nervous, because if the department failed, the leader would be replaced, and the ship would not be able to proceed for its assigned cruise. This would also mean that the carrier we were to relieve in the Pacific could not come home until *Ranger* was retested and passed.

Fortunately, *Ranger* passed with flying colors, air operations included. We were given an "above average" score for being capable of bringing the air wing aircraft back on board during night and all-weather operations. As we sailed into Pearl Harbor, all hands (or sailors), dressed in their whites, lined the deck as we honored the USS

Arizona, which was bombed and sunk by the Japanese on December 1, 1941. This was the start of the US involvement in WWII, the big war. On the *Arizona*, there remain many sailors whose bodies were not removed at the request of their families. Your grandfather was on the bridge, starting my qualifications as command duty officer underway, which meant I was learning to drive a ship, not an airplane. It took some time to learn that a seventy-six-thousand-ton ship does not respond in the same way a small aircraft responds. However, most aviators transition very well since they are used to judging relative motion.

At this point, I need to share with you regarding my spiritual walk. Except for my prayer for Matt's life to be spared, for the men lost in the Oriskany fire and for grandmother's surgery, your grandmother and I were what many call "nominal Christians." We believed and would go to church on special days, but neither of us had a personal relationship with Jesus. Just prior to leaving VAQ-135, Betty and I had our most difficult time in our marriage because I lacked a Christian undergirding and was so very prideful about being the commanding officer of VAQ-135. The squadron came first in my prideful life, before my wife and my children. I am convinced today that the Lord knew I needed to be away from home, so he sent me to sea on the *Ranger*.

Weeks later, after arriving in Subic Bay in the Philippines, I received a letter from a very excited wife, who shared that she was now a born-again Christian. Grandmother also shared that she had been led to the Lord by a dear neighbor, Tibby Coffee, and that the wife of my previous VAQ-135 operations officer, Lucia Helms, had also accepted Christ at the same charismatic ministry event. Since VAQ-135 was embarked on *Ranger*, this called for a serious discussion with her husband, Hugh. Commander Helms suggested that I contact the chaplain if I had a religious question. Betty also indicated that Lucia and family had been a special help to her even thought I was no longer the skipper. As you know, we have maintained this special relationship, and she has become your Aunt Lucia. I still marvel at the love she has for you and the fun alligator stories she shares with you. Hers is just one of the many special families the Lord has allowed us to know and fellowship with along the way.

When I received Betty's news, I was not excited. In my mind, I did not need a "Jesus freak" for a wife, thinking it could hinder my professional growth—my pride. Days later, I took the letter to Jim Doffin, our Protestant chaplain and a good friend. I asked him what I should do about my crazy wife. Of all things, he asked about my relationship with Jesus! I said, "Jim, I did not come here to talk about me, but my wife, who has become a religious fanatic."

Trent, this started a journey for your grandfather that lasted until the fall of 1976, when I came to the foot of the cross at the naval chapel at Whidbey Island. However, I will share that part of my life later. First, I do need to tell you that our cruise was going so well that we were scheduled for a port visit in Hong Kong in March 1976. I was very excited, since we were able to schedule a flight for your grandmother to Hong Kong via Tokyo, Japan. I met her at the airport with one single red rose, and we crossed the harbor by ferry to the Hong Kong Hilton, where we stayed for five glorious days.

From the first time I saw her at the airport, I realized that I truly had a new wife—and you had a new grandmother, long before you arrived on the scene. She was happier and more at peace than I had seen her in our more than twenty years of marriage. I was sure she was serious about her new faith walk when we reached the hotel. In her bags, I thought she had brought me all the Christian books ever written, plus a new Bible. This showed how little I knew about the Christian faith that I professed. Of course, this prideful naval aviator had to find a brown paper bag to take them back to the ship so that my shipmates would not see what I was reading. We had a wonderful visit, and you can see a picture of us on a boat in Hong Kong harbor in my memories bookcase. It was very hard to say good-bye as we sailed back out to sea, but I was glad there were several wives who traveled together so she did not have to go to the airport by herself.

We sailed out to participate in a large Pacific Rim exercise in which we simulated the possibility of the Cold War with the Russians becoming hot. We flew night and day for over a week off the coast of the Philippines. It was good in that I was too busy to miss my family. Several weeks later, we sailed back into Subic Bay for some needed rest and relaxation.

While in port, we received word that the Iranians had taken over the American embassy in Tehran, Iraq. The *Ranger* was ordered to proceed at flank speed (as fast as the ship would go) through the straights of Melaka into the Indian Ocean. That would mean that *Ranger* would cross the equator, the zero meridian. According to navy tradition, when a sailor or officer crosses the equator, he changes from a "pollywog" to a "shellback." However, to make that passage, you must go through a ceremony conducted on the flight deck, which is not very pleasant. Since your grandfather was a pollywog and many who worked for me were shellbacks, I was not looking forward to the ceremony.

The night before we sailed, my boss, Cdr. Dave Morris, came to my stateroom to tell me that the Red Cross had sent a message to the ship that my father (Pops) was in the veterans hospital in Denver, Colorado, in critical condition, and they recommend I come home. I then took the long flight home to Kansas City, where I picked up your grandmother, had a short visit with your aunt, your uncle, and your dad, and headed for Denver. When we arrived, Pops was very sick after having a cancerous tumor removed. Grandmother and I stayed a week. Pops was getting better, so the doctor cleared us to leave, which was very difficult for me. We returned to Missouri, where I had a day to visit with my children before I started my trip back to the *Ranger*, which was now in the Indian Ocean. Seventy-two hours and over fifteen thousand miles later, I landed at a small atoll in the Indian Ocean called Diego Garcia, which is about three miles long and is owned by the British. The following day, the *Ranger* sent an aircraft to pick me up. I truly was glad to be back on board the ship.

Less than a week after my return to the ship, Commander Morris again visited my stateroom to tell me that my dad had passed away. At this point I had travel fatigue just thinking about that return trip but knew that I must be there for Pops's funeral. I was flown back to Diego

Garcia and then took a very long, fourteen-hour propeller aircraft flight to the Philippines, followed by a flight to Clark Air Force Base, where I waited for an aircraft to take me to Hawaii. In Hawaii, the plane broke down, so I went across the field to the Honolulu commercial terminal and bought a ticket to Kansas City. After five days in transit to Missouri and a ten-hour drive to Colorado, I was totally exhausted, both mentally and physically. Betty fully understood how I felt, and I did get to spend a couple of days with Matt, Debra, and Michael.

On the return trip, I flew out of Travis Air Force Base in California and found, after arriving, that the *Ranger* was returning from the Indian Ocean and was south of the equator, not far from Singapore. When I arrived in Singapore, there was a Carrier Onboard Deliver (COB) aircraft at the airport ready to fly out to the *Ranger*. The COD aircraft are the people, parts, and mail planes for the carriers. I found the pilot and asked him what the location of the ship was, and he said it was south of the equator. There was no way I was going to return with this flight, with 2,999 shellbacks on board and one pollywog. The next day, when I checked with the COD pilot, the ship had crossed to north of the equator during the night. I knew they would not turn the ship around just for one pollywog, so I gladly jumped on board and returned to my home at sea. On board, I found a note that Commander Morris wanted to see me.

After expressing his condolences regarding my father, he asked, "Did you really delay your flight from Singapore until the ship had crossed the equator?"

I then found out the COD pilot had squealed on me, and I had to say, "Yes, sir, I did."

He then handed me an engraved name tag that read "Senior Slimy Pollywog" and said, "You will wear this for the rest of the cruise." Inwardly, I smiled, since I would be happy to wear this rather than go through the awful ceremony.

USS *Ranger* would complete one more exercise in the Sea fo Japan before being relieved by the USS *Independence* and heading home. We passed the *Independence* as it was headed for the Indian Ocean because our embassy in Tehran was still under siege. In route home, I was promoted to operations officer, the department head position, even though I was a "slimy pollywog." The operations officer was the number-three position on the ship, and I had completed all the requirements to be a command duty officer underway, having brought the carrier into port and commanded the ship for alongside underway replenishment with a tanker where fuel, food and supplies were brought aboard. Both of these tasks were difficult with a seventy-six-thousand-ton ship.

I was very excited as we approached Hawaii, knowing that my son Matt and many other ship force sons would meet the ship and sail home from Hawaii with us. Unfortunately, Michael was too young to make the flight. Needless to say, we had a wonderful five days, and Matt learned all about *Ranger* and watched the fly-off as we approached San Diego. After docking, Matt and I were excited to head to an airport for our flight home.

After a thirty-day leave period, I returned to San Diego, where the *Ranger's* mission for carrier qualification training was. As the operations officer, I was very busy with the flight schedule and the operation of the ship. As mentioned earlier, the USS *Ranger* was scheduled for an overhaul at the naval shipyard in Bremerton, Washington, starting in the fall of 1976. There is much planning required in moving a ship with two thousand sailors on board, since logistically we would transport as many of the crew and their families as possible, along with their automobiles, to the new home port. For a ship that at that time had no women on board, plans had to be made to accommodate the female population, and one of the rules was that ladies could not live with their husbands. Since Betty had never been out on a carrier except for a one-day family cruise, I invited her and Michael, who was four years old, to join us for the trip north.

In the fall of 1976, the USS *Ranger* departed San Diego with over five hundred automobiles on the flight deck and over one thousand family members on board for this three-day sail to Bremerton. We started the short cruise with an immediate crisis for the operations officer. One of the requirements for a ship going into the shipyard is to burn down the over one million gallons of the distillate fuel marine, which fuels everything on the ship, to the lowest level possible. This way, there would be little to offload upon arrival at Bremerton. Fuel is stored in many different tanks so that, if the ship is targeted and hit, not all the fuel supply will be lost.

On a diesel-powered ship like the *Ranger*, the only way to know how much fuel you have on board is to manually dip all of your tanks. Late on the first night at sea, just off Los Angeles, the captain called me to the bridge (where the ship is controlled) for an emergency meeting. On the way to the bridge, I passed a sailor dipping a fuel tank who, not knowing I was listening, said in rather colorful at sea language, "This is the [blank- blank] twentieth time I have dipped this tank and reported back!"

Instantly, I had some idea what our emergency was. When I arrived on the bridge, the captain advised me that the engineering officer (EO) had miscalculated our remaining fuel, and we did not have enough fuel to reach the Puget Sound area. When a ship runs out of fuel, it is an extreme emergency, because the ship not only loses propulsion but almost all of the utilities as well. With over one thousand guests on board, including my wife and my four-year-old son, this was serious. We first checked to see if there were any navy oilers in the area so we could do an underway replenishment, but there were none.

Our only other choice would be to steam into the San Francisco harbor, tie up at Alameda Naval Air Station, which had carrier piers, and take on fuel. This would be a logistical nightmare since it would require a complete port entry request, including harbor pilots, tugboats, and special permits. This would also be a huge embarrassment to the ship—especially the captain. The captain, in an understandably foul mood, dismissed us and told us he wanted a recommendation by six in the morning.

Commander Fox and I departed and proceeded to engineering control, where we would spend the next five hours working on this critical decision. At 5:00 a.m., after looking at all our options, we both agreed, for safety reasons, on the decision to go into port. As I headed out to go to the bridge, another thought occurred to me. I am unsure why I did not think of this before that point, but I asked the EO how much aviation jet fuel he had on board— five hundred thousand gallons, he said.

"Will it work in your boilers?" I asked.

"They do not like us to use it since it burns so hot," he said, "but it will work."

With only a few minutes remaining, we finally had our solution: we would proceed to Bremerton, and, if we did not have enough fuel, we would use the jet fuel as emergency fuel. The captain was very pleased, complimented us on our work, and said, "Why did I not think of that?" At six fifteen, I dropped, exhausted, into my bunk, only to receive a wakeup call at eight from your dad, announcing it was time to go to breakfast.

The rest of the trip was uneventful, and Betty, Michael, and our other civilian passengers enjoyed it very much. We were able to arrange a fly-by with the jets from Air Wing Sixteen, the *Ranger*'s air wing when deploying to the Pacific. One night at sea, Betty and I were invited to the captain's quarters, which was a special treat since the captain always had better food and gourmet cooks. I had asked my electronic maintenance officer, Angus McClain, to babysit our son while we dined with the captain. After dinner, when we found Angus, we asked Michael what he and Angus had done. He said, "I had a great time, and after dinner, Angus took me up on the mast of the ship!" Betty almost fainted, since the mast was a good 150 feet above the island, but Michael had loved it! Another aspect of the ship that Michael loved was the helicopter that we were required to have on the flight deck in case of emergencies, such as someone falling overboard.

Trent, your dad loved that helicopter and would spend hours sitting in the pilot's seat, pretending to fly the helicopter. I think you have seen the picture of him in the pilot's seat.

Late on the third day, we sailed into beautiful Puget Sound, with its magnificent view of Seattle, Mount Olympus, and Mount Baker, around the Olympic Peninsula to Bremerton Naval Ship Yard, and into our assigned dry dock. It was so late when we arrived that we did not off-load the passengers, crew, or cars until the following day. They would not commence the overhaul for at least a month after draining the dry dock and performing necessary defueling and maintenance on the ship. We arrived with about five hours of DFM fuel remaining and were complimented on having so little fuel in our tanks, our superiors not having any idea of the crisis we had gone through. All on board enjoyed the trip except for a few who spent time in sickbay for seasickness. Since we had my San Diego car on the flight deck, when the offload was complete, Betty, Michael, and I departed, using two ferries to reach Whidbey Island and our home in Oak Harbor. Matt and Debra were delighted to see us.

When I returned to the ship the following Monday, the Captain called and asked me come to his cabin. I am glad I was seated, since Captain McCrimmon was going to ask me if I would become the ship's force operational maintenance officer in charge of the entire $1.5 million overhaul. I first jokingly asked him if I had a choice, and he said that I did, but he would very much like me to accept. What other choice did I have? So off to overhaul school I would go at the shipyard. We immediately set up an overhaul operations center, which I ran, tracking every single event in the overhaul. Since the *Ranger* was scheduled to depart Bremerton in one year, the schedule was critical.

With my family on Whidbey Island, I was commuting via two ferries on the weekend. Later, while in the shipyard, the new air operations officer Commander Dick Gunderman, who had relieved me as CO of VAQ-135, bought a Cessna 135, and I was able to fly back and forth with Dick when the weather allowed. Shortly after taking over the new overhaul position, I was selected to be promoted to captain, which is the same rank as the CO of *Ranger*. Since I was scheduled to depart *Ranger* in 1977, I was once again faced with a major career decision. I could go to sea again and leave my family, or I could ask for a shore assignment, which would ensure that I did not make admiral.

Although I did not know it, I was also about to end my spiritual search, two days before my oldest son Matt would graduate from high school and two days before my forty-second birthday.

The overhaul was going well, and I was doing a lot of driving so I could also be home with my family. Every weekend I was home, my wife would ask when was I going to become a Christian. I did not appreciate this, since all along I had thought I was okay. However, I was watching the changed lives of many of our friends. There was a lay-witness program at the base chapel where several people from the East Coast paid their own airfare just to share with our church family about what Jesus was doing in their lives. I was sure we had paid their airfare, but the organizer of the program, my wife, assured me that all we had provided for them were families to stay with and meals. This event convinced me that what my wife, your grandmother, had experienced was real and had truly changed her life. I also now know that the Holy Spirit was working on your grandfather.

On Friday, June 3, 1977, I was serving as the command duty officer (CDO) on board *Ranger* and was responsible for everything that took place during that 24-hour period. At the same time, I was reading Chuck Colson's book *Born Again*, one of the books Betty had given me in Hong Kong. At ten that evening, I went up to the flight deck to make sure everything was secure. Normally at that hour there is no one there. However, that night there was one lone sailor walking the deck. I had never seen him on the ship, but he approached me and addressed me as "Commander Maxwell." "Sir, could I ask you a question?" he asked.

I answered, "Sure, young man."

He then said, "Sir, are you a Christian?"

I am not sure how I answered, but I was wondering how he could ask a senior officer such a personal question. I do know that I did not sleep very well that night. Your grandmother said I was wrestling with the Lord.

I was relieved at 8:00 a.m. Saturday morning and headed home to Whidbey Island and my family. I crossed Puget Sound on the Keystone Ferry and drove north to catch the Mukilteo Ferry, which connects to

Whidbey Island. Parked in the ferry waiting lot, I was continuing to read Chuck's book *Born Again*. I was at a part of the book where Chuck shares that, after Watergate, he had flown to the Northeast to visit a good friend, the CEO of Raytheon. Tom Phillips told Chuck he needed to ask Christ into his life, something Chuck was not ready to address. Leaving Tom's house late that night, he sat in his car, alone, and realized that pride was keeping him from addressing the Christian faith. With this realization, he broke down crying so hard that he could not drive.

As I sat in the ferry lot, the ferry arrived, and cars started to drive on the ferry. Like Chuck, I was now profusely crying and trying to drive, realizing my pride was keeping me from accepting Christ. I was the last car not to get on the ferry and was stopped, in my uniform, with tears running down my face. The ferry attendant came up to my car and said, "Sir, please do not be so upset—there will be another ferry along in fifteen minutes!" I am sure when he went home that evening he told his wife he had a navy commander in the ferry line who was crying because he missed the ferry. He could not have known that my life would soon be radically changed.

Matt had accepted Christ shortly before I had returned from the cruise, and Debra would join us later, in Germany. The day after I sat crying as I waited for a ferry was Sunday, June 5, 1977. During a simple communion service at the base chapel, I went forward and committed my life to Jesus Christ. Back at home, I shared with Betty, "I finally did it."

"You did what?" she asked.

I told her what I had done but that I did not think He had accepted me, because nothing had happened. She quickly explained to me why nothing had happened and once again shared her commitment day with me, although some days after her commitment, Betty did receive confirmation in a dream from Psalm 40. This started a remarkable journey, which I am, praise the Lord, still on. I have also been asked if I believe in angels, since in the following six months on board *Ranger*, I never again saw the sailor I had met on the flight deck Friday evening.

I returned to the ship as what I now know as a new man in Christ: "Therefore if anyone be in Christ he is a new creation, the old has gone the new has come" (2 Corinthians 5:17 NASB). I was more at peace with myself, and things were definitely better at home. As changes occur, we do not always realize they have taken place. The first thing the Holy Spirit did was to remove my bad sailor language. You see, in the late 1970s, there were no women on board our ships, so sometime we used poor language. After about a month, my assistant asked one day if he could have a private meeting with me.

We stepped across the passageway to my stateroom, and John asked, "Sir, what has happened to you?"

"What did you mean by that question?" I answered.

"I have not heard you say one bad word for the last month," he said.

I did not realize this had even happened. Being a very new Christian, I was not sure what to tell John, but after what seemed like a long time, I said, "John, I have accepted Jesus Christ as my Lord and Savior."

He was absolutely dumbfounded and said, "Thank you, sir."

I am certain that that was not the answer he had been expecting. However, it was a wonderful opportunity to plant some seeds in this very professional, hard-driving fighter pilot.

I realized I was approaching my six-month to depart the USS Ranger, and I was going to have to make a decision on my next duty station. Now that I had been selected as captain, my next career move would be to consider a Pentagon tour with the navy department and see if I would be selected for a deep draft command, which would require me to be command officer of an oiler for a year, followed by taking command of an aircraft carrier. I soon realized that this career selection would take me away from my family again, this time for possibly two years. Much prayer, now on a new level, led me to research another possible career direction. While talking with my assignment officer, I found out that the position of naval attaché to the Federal Republic of Germany would be opening up in a little over a year. One year in language school and then a move to Bonn, Germany, would work well with my rotation. After prayer, I asked that my application be submitted to the Department of State for consideration. Within a month, my assignment officer called and informed me that I had been accepted.

The next step was to choose where I would like to attend language school. My options were the Foreign Service Institute (FSI) in Washington, where most state department employees attended, or the Defense Language Institute (DLS) in Monterey, California. Location would have had us choose Monterey, but the DLS taught students to read and understand German, while the FSI taught students to speak German. So we chose Washington's FSI. In addition to completing my overhaul work, I was looking for new opportunities to better understand my new faith commitment. With the help of the Navigators, a Christian missionary organization, my understanding of my faith continued to grow. Additionally, we signed up for a revival in Oregon called Jesus Northwest. So with Betty, Debra, Matt, and Michael, I headed south. Once at the revival, we experienced great joy from the music and teachings. We all split up, Grandma taking Michael to a children's program while she went to an adult teaching with Matt and Debra.

I was truly frightened when we again found Betty, who was crying profusely. I said, "What in the world at this joyful revival caused this?" Well, Betty had taken Michael to a children's program, which was a clown ministry. As a young boy, Michael was deathly frightened of clowns. Knowing this, she was concerned. At the end of the program, when the clown asked the children to come forward and give their hearts to Jesus, without any coaching, your dad went forward and repeated the Sinner's Prayer. Betty was so overcome with joy that she couldn't stop crying. On the gleeful ride home, I said, "What a wonderful weekend—and also very inexpensive!" Then Debra reminded me that I had purchased over $200 of Christian material.

A lay-witness program trip to Juneau, Alaska, came shortly after the revival. I had been so impressed with the Christian lay witness at our church that I wanted to also be a part of a program. The trip to Alaska was wonderful and spiritual, and I learned much about my new faith. During my last night there, I was assigned as a leader for a small group of ladies as we concluded with reflections on the visit. One of the ladies in my group shared about a time when her husband was very sick mentally, and as she walked in her garden and expressed her concern to the Lord, He lit up the flowers on the walkway. One of the other ladies turned and told me, "I have been a Christian my entire life, and the Lord had never done that for me. Why not?"

Being such a new Christian, I had absolutely no answer for her. It was clear that the Holy Spirit was working in the room when one of the other ladies turned and asked if she had children, and she said yes. "Then," the lady said, "do you treat any of your children the same? You must understand that our Lord also never treats his children the same."

Needless to say, I said a "Thank you, Lord!" under my breath. We stayed with a wonderful couple who lived where the salmon swim upstream to mate, which was fascinating to watch. The entire trip was a true blessing and a real encouragement in my new walk with the Lord.

At a wonderful farewell party in Bremerton, I was able to share that duty on *Ranger* had been, to date, my most challenging assignment—and that, since I'd had the honor of working with such professionals, it had been my best assignment as well. I also shared about the event in the Whidbey chapel in June and how it had changed my life and urged each person present to look into their Christian calling. My assistant told me that night that he finally understood. It is important for us understand that our challenge, scripturally, is to plant the seeds, and others, with the help of the Holy Spirit, will water and harvest.

CHAPTER 10

Becoming a German-Speaking Diplomat

We were all very excited as we moved to Washington, DC, in preparation for our new assignment. In addition to attending the Foreign Service Institute to learn German, I would be required to attend the Attaché School, taught by the Defense Intelligence Agency (DIA), which I would be working for. I would also have classes with the Central Intelligence Agency, which I would be collaborating with in my new position. Since we assumed that I would be returning to the Pentagon following my Bonn assignment, we purchased a house in Springfield, Virginia, just outside Washington.

Because Debra had graduated from high school, she was allowed to attend language school with us. None of the family had any idea how difficult learning a new language was going to be. Since our commute was close to forty-five minutes, we did have the added advantage of speaking German all the way to school and back home. Frau Stambach, our German instructor, was very demanding and required us to study very hard. She had written the famous line for President Kennedy when he visited the Berlin Wall: "Ich bin ein Berliner," which means, "I am a Berliner." The final exam was most difficult, but all three of us passed with the grade of three for speaking and two for reading. Fives in speaking and reading indicated fluency as a native German.

I also determined that the German Navy's ships were the US Navy's Adams-class destroyers. A request to the Department of the Navy found an Adams-class destroyer coming out of overhaul in Boston and headed to its homeport in Norfolk, Virginia. I was not ready for the commanding officer to ask me if I would be their acting commodore for the trip south. The skipper wanted to train his crew for when the actual commodore boarded the ship in Norfolk as commander of the destroyer squadron. I would be performing all the duties of the commodore during the five-day trip from Boston to Norfolk.

I was truly treated like royalty and picked up at the airport by an official car and driver and driven to the shipyard and piped aboard as a commodore, or honorary admiral. My stateroom was large and plush for a small ship. The first day out was very routine until close to sunset, when the ship conducted a burial at sea for a retired naval officer. The officer of the deck (OOD) called and asked, "Sir, would you please join us on the fantail [or stern] for the burial-at-sea ceremony?" I then became a part of a beautiful and thoughtful ceremony, which was filmed and sent to the next of kin.

I returned to my stateroom and was preparing for dinner when the OOD called and asked permission to fire on the coffin. I was certainly not prepared for this and immediately called the skipper to find out what in the world we were doing. He explained that though the coffin is prepared with holes in it so that it will sink, it sometimes does not, and to remove any chance of it becoming a hazard, the ship's marksmen must shoot and sink the coffin. I gave the OOD permission but made sure this was not filmed. The remainder of the trip was routine, and we arrived in Norfolk to much fanfare, since the ship was coming home. During this trip, I learned much about the capability of the Adams-class destroyer.

My classes with the DIA and the CIA were very interesting since the Cold War with Russia was ongoing. My last training was the CIA driving course south of Washington. This was a little like a demolition derby. We were taught how to run a roadblock if the bad guys ever tried to stop us while we were driving without our chauffeur. The final test was at night, and we had to navigate on narrow roads and pass through six attempts to stop our forward travel. My car made it but was a total wreck as I approached the finish line.

We now felt we were ready for our new assignment in Bonn, West Germany. We put all of our household belongings in storage, since our Bonn home would be furnished, rented out our Springfield home, and headed for the airport. We flew into the air force base in Frankfurt, where we were met by a car and a delightful gentleman named Franz Dzbas, who would become my driver for the next three years. Once on the Autobahn, which has no speed limit, we drove to Bonn at speeds of up to ninety miles an hour. Betty did not like it; however, Michael thought it was cool.

Given our overnight flight and the six-hour time difference between the East Coast and Bonn, we arrived in Bonn exhausted. We were housed in the diplomatic guesthouse since the current naval attaché was still living in the home we would occupy. Some very kind folks from the embassy had provided all of our immediate needs, including some German food that we had never eaten. We were settled and preparing to take a nap when the doorbell rang. Capt. Bill Campbell, the officer I would relieve, and his wife had come to welcome us to Bonn, bearing beautiful flowers and inviting us to diner at their (soon to become our) home. Over the next several hours, everyone in the attaché office came by to welcome us to Bonn. We did not know it at the time, but the best way to get over jet lag in one day is not to go to bed until evening the day you arrive. I later found out that the mission of the defense attaché office that day was to make sure we did not go to bed until bedtime. They were very successful: that evening we dropped, exhausted, into our beds and awoke in the morning with no jet lag.

Within days, I had checked into the defense attaché's office in the American embassy, which was protected by a high electric fence and US Marines with automatic weapons. I was immediately scheduled for briefings with the embassy security detail and the members of the Central Intelligence Agency staff. All briefings were top secret or above and given in "the bubble," which was an airtight room where it is impossible to monitor conversations from outside. In my three years at the embassy, I would attend many meetings in the bubble. It was immediately clear that my new assignment was going to involve a number of clandestine efforts.

My predecessor, Captain Campbell, set up a schedule for me to present my credentials to the head of the German Navy and my German Navy liaison officer, who worked in the intelligence section. The entire interview with the German Chief of Naval Operations was in German, and I departed feeling as if I was going home soon since I only understood about twenty to thirty percent of the conversation. Bill told me that they always did that to determine the language capability of the new attaché. I did understand when the admiral asked if I was ready to assume this important US Navy position.

Since I would be the principal naval advisor to the ambassador to the Federal Republic of Germany, Ambassador Arthur Burns, I was then scheduled for an appointment to meet the ambassador. Ambassador Burns was a gracious and kind individual and knew Chuck Colson from his Washington days—and was even in Chuck's book *Born Again*. After he shared with me what he had expected from the Naval Attaché, we had an encouraging conversation about Chuck, not knowing that during my tour, I would meet Chuck in Germany. In addition to our official meetings, I would meet with my boss, the army attaché. I also met again with my driver, Franz, to set some travel ground rules, including one stating that Autobahn speeds would not exceed eighty miles per hour, which he was not too happy about. Because a terrorist group was operating in Germany, we were also at times carrying concealed weapons and wearing flax vests. Within the last year, the army attaché in France had been shot and killed.

The assignment called for the attachés to support intelligence gathering on the Soviet Union and the Soviet Bloc countries, represent the US Navy at official functions, authorize and approve US Navy ship visits to Germany, and be the principle embassy advisor on the US Navy. Michael started school at the Bonn American School across the street from our home, and we immediately joined the American Protestant Church, which was also within walking distance from our home. As very new Christians, we were anxious to meet other Christians in the

community. We immediately started to fellowship with the d...
Campus Crusade for Christ and the Navigator families. I wa...
support both their ministries behind the Iron Curtain in the
Union and will share about that later.

Since my position involved a lot of entertaining, our family h...
delightful Filipino maid named Tessie, who would be our maid for...
three years in Bonn. In addition to a maid, I was assigned an interpret...
who would come to my office one hour each week to continue to hel...
me with my German. Most mornings I could ride my bike along a
bike path by the Rhine river to work. In addition to my office work, I
had to start scheduling visits to German naval bases and air stations in
Northern Germany. The superintendent of the German naval academy
invited us to make a formal visit to his school. The superintendent,
Admiral Steindorf, had previously been the German Naval Attaché in
Washington, and he and his wife had become our friends while we were
in language school. We were treated like royalty and enjoyed our visit
with the Admiral, our US Navy representative and some of the students.
I was pleased to get to know the admiral better, something that would
help during some difficult dealings I would have with him later.

I truly believe I could write an entire journal about our tour in
Germany, but I will just write about a few of the most memorable events
that took place during those three years. Betty and I had some very sad
and exciting Christian experiences in Germany. We became very close
with two couples in particular: Paul and Phyllis Stanley, a European
Navigator family, and Bob and Marilyn Ehle, a diplomatic ministry
team from Campus Crusade for Christ. These two families taught two
very new Christians much about their walk with the Lord.

One of the most difficult things we would face with our friends was
the death of Marilyn and Bob's son Rickie of cancer, two days after he
graduated from Bonn High School. Marilyn, Bob, and Rick taught us
so very much about how Christians deal with adversity. Three years
before Rick's death, he wrote in his diary, "I acknowledge the total
claim that Jesus Christ has on my life as His child. I hereby affirm that
I am making myself available to Him to: Go anywhere He wants me

to go, say anything He wants me to say, give away anything He wants me to give and do anything He wants me to do. I surrender my will to His Lordship over my life in trust that whatever He asks of me He will create in me the desire and ability to accomplish through His indwelling Holy Spirit."

Trent, you cannot imagine what a positive impact this made on your new Christian grandparents. Thirty-three years later, I still carry Ricky's testimony in my Bible so I can share with inmates I minister to about how to deal with difficulties in our Christian walk.

Bob and Marilyn were also responsible for an answered prayer for me. When we left Washington state for Germany, via Washington, DC, the lady who had led Grandmother to the Lord, Tibby Coffee, made your grandfather promise that I would place on my daily prayer list the opportunity to meet Chuck Colson, since his book *Born Again* was so influential in my conversion. I told her that was foolish since I was going to Germany and Chuck lived in Naples, Florida, but she insisted. So on my daily prayer list was to meet Chuck Colson! Two years into our tour in Bonn, Bob and Marilyn Ehle called and asked if we would have a reception in our home for a visiting Christian who was in ministry. We had a nice home and had entertained other visitors in the past, so I responded and said, "Certainly, who is the visitor?" I was totally shocked when Bob told me Chuck Colson, and I realized this was an answer to my prayer! While introducing Chuck at the event, I said, "If you place things on your prayer list, be sure you understand that, even if difficult, they might just walk in your front door." Chuck was free the following day, so Franz and I had the honor of showing him Bonn, the capital of Germany at the time. This started a wonderful and meaningful thirty-year relationship that I will share with you later.

Paul and Phyllis Stanley were also in diplomatic ministry and were more involved with ministry behind the Iron Curtain in Russia. Each week, a sealed diplomatic van would leave Bonn, Germany, for Moscow with classified material for the embassy. I developed a relationship with the naval attaché in Russia and asked if I could send him Christian Navigator material for use there. Although I did not know if he was a believer, he was pleased to help us because of our friendship. Since the Navigators teach one-on-one discipleship, the material was well suited for work with smaller numbers in places where large Christian worship services weren't possible. I would load a large briefcase full of Christian discipleship material and put it into the sealed van. Because of diplomatic immunity, the Soviets could not open the van to inspect what was inside. On arrival at the embassy in Moscow, the briefcase was delivered to the naval attaché. Some weeks later, Paul or another Navigator would travel to the Soviet Union on a civilian passport and go to the American embassy carrying an identical empty briefcase. In an almost James Bond–like manner, the Navigator would report to the naval attaché's office and exchange the empty briefcase for a briefcase full of Christian Navigator discipleship material. The pickup team then had a special house designated as a drop house, where the material would be taken for a Navigator in Russia to pick up and then take to the station where it would be distributed and used.

This system resulted in an amazing story of God moving. On one delivery, when Paul was doing the embassy pickup, the naval attaché was absent, and the office staff knew nothing about the delivery. After at least an hour and a phone call to the embassy in Bonn, the exchange took place. Paul expedited his departure, knowing that the timing for the delivery to the pickup house was critical, since there was reason to believe the Soviet Intelligence Service was following the Christians. When Paul arrived at the pickup house, the occupants told him he had missed the pickup by half an hour. Paul sat down for a snack, having no idea what he was going to do with the material since the pickup houses, for security purposes, were never the same. After a brief time of sharing and prayer with the occupants, Paul was preparing to leave to return the material to the embassy when there was a knock on the door. The Russian family, thinking it might be the Soviet Intelligence Service, hid Paul in their attic. He was much relieved when the family came and led him to their living room to meet a man who, as he told Paul, was from Siberia and had taken a train for five days to Moscow. During a small house church service in Siberia, the worshippers had been told by the Holy Spirit that if they would go to a certain address in Moscow, there would be a man there who would have some Christian discipleship material for them to use in Siberia. After many "Praise the Lord"s and much prayer, the man departed, opening up the Navigator ministry in Siberia.

I want to share one other faith-building story, among many, from my time in Bonn. Since I was briefed almost weekly regarding the Soviet Secret Service (SSS), I was asked by the Navigator staff working inside the Soviet Union if I would come to Vienna, Austria, to give a two-day seminar on the unclassified makeup and operation of the SSS and how it could affect their Christian operations inside Russia. Since it had been some time since Betty had visited Vienna, she and Michael were going to join me. As we approached the time to depart, a conflict came up regarding a school program for your dad, and they could not accompany me. Once this change of plans was reported to the Navigator team, they changed my arrival point to a small town short of Vienna.

Since I was often shadowed by Soviet agents, an elaborate arrival plan was devised and hand-delivered to me in Bonn by the Stanleys. My instructions were to go up to the information desk after my train's arrival and inquire about a bus to Vienna. This was the sign for the pickup team to ensure that I was not being followed and that it was your grandfather and not someone else they were picking up. After visiting the information desk, I was to cross the street, wait for a yellow VW beetle to come around the corner and stop, and jump in.

Now, you need to understand that German trains are never late and run almost to the second for departures and arrivals. Never while in Germany did I ever experience an early or late train—except my train to Austria that day. Once I was securely in the passenger seat of the VW, the driver raced off. The Navigator in the back seat then began to share a God story with us as we headed for a clandestine location. They had arrived some twenty minutes before the scheduled arrival time, and the driver had remained in the car while the passenger stepped into a coffee bar. Once he was in the Austrian coffee shop, an American young lady came in and sat down next to him. During the conversation, she relayed that she was a Christian and had married an Austrian in the United States. Shortly after their return to Austria, he was drafted into the Austrian Army. She was left with his parents, who spoke no English. At the point of desperation, she prayed that if she was going to make it, she needed to talk to an American who could counsel and encourage her. Since my family couldn't travel with me and my train was thirty minutes late, this was God answering her prayer. The Navigator was able to counsel, encourage, and pray with her because he was in the right town and had extra time. What a mighty God we serve!

The weekend was great, and I learned much about the commitment of the Navigators to distribute the message behind the Iron Curtain. On Sunday, before departing, I was taken to another safe house to brief the Campus Crusade Soviet ministry.

One other experience for your dad was that when the pope visited Bonn in 1980, he stayed down the street at the Vatican embassy, and your dad waited for hours to see him come by in his lighted pope mobile.

Among the many events that we experienced while in Bonn were certainly many very memorable experiences. Several involved my work with the ambassador to the Federal Republic of Germany, Arthur Burns, who had been head of the Federal Reserve for President Eisenhower. In the fall of each year, Germany has a large naval celebration in Kiel. Navy ships from around the world sail there to celebrate Kiel week. In 1981, we were the escorts for the US ambassador and Mrs. Burns as they represented the United States in Kiel.

The ambassador, his wife, and Betty and I visited the US Navy host ship, and afterward we attended the impressive and royal banquet that concluded the Kiel week celebration. During the dinner, a German Navy staff aide advised me that there was an important phone call in the kitchen for Ambassador Burns. Since I was his escort and did not want to interrupt his dinner, I went to the kitchen to take the call and if necessary carry a message to the ambassador. Reaching the phone, I said, "This is Captain Maxwell, Ambassador Burn's escort. Could I take a message for the ambassador, who is having dinner?"

The individual on the line said, "This is President Reagan, and I need to talk to the ambassador."

My immediate answer was "Yes, sir, Mr. President. I will get him immediately"—which I did. Later in the evening, I asked the ambassador if he could share what the president had needed. He was kind enough to tell me that the Russians wanted to build an oil pipeline across Germany to the Atlantic Ocean, and he needed the Ambassador's input before making a major decision. It was a critical piece in the president's eventual decision to support the construction of the pipeline.

It was also my privilege to be the escort for Ambassador Burns while he visited the USS *Eisenhower* operating in the Mediterranean Sea off Italy. We flew by a VIP aircraft from Bonn to the naval air station in Naples. Normally, VIPs are flown in carrier onboard delivery (COD) aircraft, a Grumman C-2 aircraft that delivers personnel and supplies to the ship daily when the ship is having flight operations. Due to the ambassador's age, which at the time was eighty, the navy decided to deliver him to the ship by helicopter so no arrested landing would be involved.

On landing, we were met by the ship captain and the carrier division commander, a rear admiral. The admiral had moved to his at sea cabin on the flag bridge so that the ambassador could have his in port more plush living spaces. Following an exceptional lunch, the ambassador was given a series of intensive briefings on every aspect of the ship's operation. At around four, we were escorted to the captain's bridge to watch two hours of air operations. We then returned to the admiral's quarters to freshen up for dinner with the admiral, who had his own mess and stewards.

At around eight in the evening of a very long day, I was more than ready to retire. However, the ambassador wanted to visit the enlisted men where they had their meals. A quick call to the bridge brought the command master chief to the admiral's stateroom to escort the ambassador to the mess deck, where he spent at least two hours talking to and encouraging the sailors of the *Eisenhower*. As I escorted the ambassador back to the admiral cabin around 11:00 p.m., I was exhausted and more than ready to, as we say in the navy, "hit the sack." I remember thanking the Lord that evening for the men on the ship who made the sacrifice to leave their families so that our way of life could be protected and for an American ambassador who cared enough to go to the enlisted mess deck to encourage the men who were serving our nation.

The next morning, we had an early breakfast, took a trip to the engineering spaces, and then visited the ship's TV studio. In the studio, Ambassador Burns gave the most impressive presentation to the entire ship's company about what it meant to serve our nation on the USS *Eisenhower*. Having served President Eisenhower as head of the Federal Reserve, he talked without notes about the complete integrity of the president and how important it was for all on board to also serve their mission with integrity. It was a very moving speech given from his heart and was deeply appreciated by the captain and his leadership team. We were given an impressive farewell on the flight deck and then headed to Naples to catch our VIP flight home. Once we were airborne, I could not help but be thankful that the United States had such a remarkable individual as our ambassador to Germany. Since many of my peers knew of my relationship with Ambassador Burns and of his Jewish faith, they would call me and ask if at official functions they could read from the New Testament. Knowing that he had attended a Christian Bible study at the White House, I would always say absolutely.

One of the most difficult Christian presentations I gave while the naval attaché was to a large group of German bankers, when I shared my testimony *auf Deutsch*—in German. After I wrote my testimony in English, my interpreter, Frau Tosha, translated it into German, and then for many weeks I worked on giving the presentation to my instructor. After many weeks, Frau Tosha cleared me to make the presentation. Since she had heard my testimony many times, I asked her if she now understood how to become a born-again Christian. She said, "Sure, just pay your 10 percent to the church, and you will be okay." She had completely missed the born-again process.

It helps to understand that Germans are very private about their religion and very uncomfortable when talking about their faith. When Chuck Colson brought his book *Born Again* to Germany, the German publisher had him change the name to *Watergate as Seen from Another Prospective*. In spite of this barrier, the bankers in Stuttgart responded very well to my testimony. Questions following the presentation were difficult, but an interpreter was present to assist me. Following the meeting, many present shared with me that they were believers. Additionally during my tour I gave the German version of Chuck's book to several admirals I worked with, and most of them later thanked me and said they had gotten a better perspective on Watergate, also missing Chuck's conversion. I again had to rest in the fact that our job is to plant the seeds and that others would reap the harvest.

In addition to long hours I spent in the office, I, accompanied by Betty, was often out in the evening representing the navy at social functions, some of which were awesome (like attending the opera), and others very boring. It was a blessing to have a social secretary in the office to take care of all of our official engagements. There were many military operations that I do not feel comfortable talking about, but some events I enjoy sharing with you and my family. One of the most exciting for your grandmother and me was our cruise up into the Baltic.

When we first arrived in Bonn, there was an all-attaché conference in London, England, which was very well attended and provided a great opportunity to visit London. At the conference, a friend, the naval attaché to Russia, approached me with a request. At that time, during the Cold War, there were many military areas of Russia that he was prohibited from visiting. One of the areas was the submarine base in northwest Russia, near Leningrad. There was, however, a ship channel that passed by the sub base as the commercial ships sailed into Leningrad. His request was for our Bonn office to purchase cruise tickets on a Norwegian cruise ship that had a port of call in Leningrad. This way, we could book their passage without the Soviets knowing of their travel. The attachés and their wives would travel with a couple from a friendly country, and the entire group would pose as civilian tourists.

As they passed the Russian sub base, the attachés were close enough to take pictures of these weapon systems. On one cruise, the Italian couple had to cancel, leaving a cabin on the Norwegian cruise ship paid for and open. That evening, before leaving the office, I jokingly sent a classified message to the Russian Naval attaché stating that Betty and I would be happy to fill in for the Italians. Arriving at work the following day, I was shocked that the Moscow embassy had answered, saying that if the Bonn defense attaché's office paid the fare out of our budget, they would be happy to have the Maxwells join them.

Shortly after my boss arrived in the office, I approached him with the proposal. Much to my surprise, we had some end-of-the-fiscal-year money to spend, and he immediately approved our trip. This was conveyed to Moscow, and our names were added to the cruise list. Michael was not very happy, since we would be gone three weeks, leaving him to stay with several families. One of the many very special families your dad would be with was the air attaché Colonel Ron Lord and his wife, Georgia. We were blessed to be alongside them when they both came to know Christ while in Bonn. I would also be privileged to work along this professional officer while attempting to recruit the assistant Soviet air attaché. Ron was also special to this navy file since he had flown the F-8 Crusader as an exchange pilot during the Vietnam War.

Getting the approval and being added to the cruise was the easy part, since your grandmother and I would have to travel to Wiesbaden for training on the photo equipment we would be using and then review overhead photography of the intended target. As we drove home, Franz asked if we were now going to be spies. I did not answer that difficult question, but I did know the answer.

We departed Bonn along with the Naval Attaché to Moscow and headed to Hamburg to board our luxury liner. Most of the guests were Germans. Since it was a very expensive trip, we were certainly the youngest on board, and we were also traveling with a large, five-hundred-millimeter camera that no one on the ship had. The ship was scheduled to stop in Poland, Gotland Island, Russia, Finland,

and finally Norway. Prior to departing the Bonn embassy, we received additional tasking for Poland, since the Poles were in such turmoil as they worked to throw off the communist control of the country.

Once underway to Gotland Island, we passed a Russian naval ship steaming north in the Baltic. We were able to go up near the top of the ship and shoot excellent pictures of the ship. At the captain's reception that evening, he asked if we got good pictures of the Russian ship, letting us know that he knew why we were on board. Later in the trip, we received a call from the bridge whenever there were Soviet ships in the area.

The night before our entry into the Leningrad channel, the US Naval Attaché from Moscow, his wife, grandmother and I met in our stateroom to discuss our strategy for the morning shoot of the Soviet submarine base. We were now in the northern part of the northern hemisphere, where it would be light at around 3:00 a.m. Since our expected time of passing the sub base was 4:00 a.m., we scouted out where each of us would shoot from. Your grandmother, now the spy, would shoot with one of our four cameras from our porthole. At three thirty there was not one person outside on deck as we started our shoot with a five-hundred-millimeter lens and automatic thirty-five-millimeter camera. The automatic feature of the camera was so loud I was sure it could be heard across the sub pens as I shot for at least thirty minutes.

We did find out on debrief that we obtained the first-ever pictures of a new Russian intercontinental ballistic missile being loaded into a submarine. When we finished, we had almost five hundred rolls of film. Now we would face the difficult problem of what to do with the film. Since I was an American diplomat and we were all carrying diplomatic passports, the four of us were afforded diplomatic immunity, which meant we could not be searched. We were actually carrying both regular civilian passports and diplomatic passports to be used only if we were going to be searched while we were carrying the film. So this meant that we had to carry the film on our person at all times until our arrival in Finland, where it would be delivered to the American embassy and flown back to the Defense Intelligence Agency in the United States. Since the Soviet Naval Attaché and his wife had been to Leningrad many times, they allowed your grandmother and me to go ashore while they stayed on board and watched over the film.

Since it was still a communist state, the authorities allowed the ship workers to go ashore first before the ship guests. Leaving the ship for a tour of Leningrad, Betty and I were standing in a line to clear immigrations when a guard pulled us out of line and took us into a separate building. They first looked at my civilian passport and then inspected my camera bag, which held none of the film we had taken earlier. They then asked what were we doing in Leningrad, and we answered that we were tourists visiting their country. As we were leaving to rejoin the tour, I offered to give the guard a "fly navy" bumper sticker, which he was not amused about. The tour was great and the food very bad. After a long day, we returned to the ship in preparation for getting underway.

Once back on board, we found out that the American naval attaché traveling with us had been called into one of the ship offices and asked by a Russian guard what he was doing on the cruise and why was he not going ashore. He was most likely too bold in telling the guard he did not like Russia and did not want to go on a tour. We were both convinced that the Soviets knew what we were doing. Leaving Russia, we had our formal dining night before going into Finland. It was almost comical to see Betty and the naval attaché's wife from Russia in their beautiful dresses carrying two large bags full of film. In Finland, we were met by a car and rushed to the embassy with our important bags of film. We were very pleased to finally deliver the film to the attaché office in Finland.

While in the embassy, the navy captain who was head of that office said he had one more mission for me. In addition to our cruise ship, there was a new Soviet naval cruiser visiting Finland, and it was giving tours to the local civilians. Out of all the attachés present, I was the only one who would not be recognized if I boarded the ship as a local tourist. Your grandmother, the naval attaché from Moscow, and his wife got a car and driver from the embassy, and Grandpa got a cab to pier side for a tour in Finnish from a local interpreter. Several hours later, I was back at the American embassy with some great pictures and helpful intelligence. The remainder of the cruise into Norway and back to Hamburg was delightful since we had no additional assignments.

Michael was totally delighted when we returned, and to ease the pain, I took him to the local embassy store and bought him an American radio-controlled speedboat. Within walking distance from our home was a park and a lake. Arriving at the lake, we put the speedboat in the water, and off it went. I knew that the Germans were great model boat builders and noticed that there were several on the other side of the lake. What we did not know was that before you dare put a boat in the water, you must have a German assigned frequency, and within minutes, the local harbormaster showed up to tell us that we were causing significant problems with our American boat. So Michael and I retreated, and I did not score any homecoming points with my son.

Four other memorable events while in Bonn were my involvement with the Soviet air attaché, two incidents at the German naval academy, and a trip through the Kiel Canal. During the Cold War with the Soviets, there was always an effort to recruit members of the other military to defect to the United States so they could be a source of intelligence gathering. I was recruited by one of the embassy agencies to work on an effort to have the Soviet air attaché defect to the United States. The air attaché and his wife had a young handicapped child, and in the Soviet Union at this time, the handicapped were throwaway children. A study of the current attaché showed a possibility that, if we offered extensive medical care for his young son, he would consider the possibility of defecting. In addition to medical care, there was an offer of a salary, housing, and asylum in the United States. The naval attaché was chosen so that, if the recruitment was not successful, it would not reflect badly on the current American air attaché. However, every step of the way, the air attaché Colonel Ron Lord was kept informed. Several months were devoted to developing a relationship, followed by extensive social catering to his family needs. I was given the freedom to select the time that we would ask the question. There was an elaborate plan in place to get the attaché and his family immediately out of Germany before it was known by the Soviet embassy if he gave a positive response.

One day at lunch, I ask the colonel if I could ask him a very serious question. Feeling comfortable with me, he said, in very good English, "Sure." Following the offer, he was very quiet and responded that could he think it over and talk to his wife. I was surprised that he was at least open to it. At our next meeting, he was very forthright with me and said that the Soviet military would never send an officer to an attaché position unless the officer has significant family members in the Soviet Union. When military members defected, the Soviets made it extremely difficult for their families. Also, as much as he appreciated the United States and Americans in general, accepting the offer would be an act of treason against his homeland. He thanked me profusely, and I assured him that no one would ever know of the offer.

The two naval academy events involved an incident with an Iranian naval officer and a replacement for the American naval liaison officer at the academy. While we were in Bonn, the Iranians had taken over the embassy in Tehran. An agency asked my assistance in asking the Iranian naval exchange student at the naval academy to help with information regarding the embassy takeover. This meeting was arranged through the American naval liaison officer at the German academy. The American agent drove to Flensburg for a lunch meeting with the Iranian student. Shortly after the meeting, before the lunch was complete, the student departed and said he was going to the superintendent's office to talk with Admiral Steindorf. Within the hour, I had a phone call from the admiral, who was not very happy with his attaché friend. His request, most reasonably, was that if we ever again needed this kind of assistance, to please let him know so he could assist us.

The last incident involved the incoming US naval liaison officer for the German naval academy. At that time, the Germans had no women serving in the armed services. The officer proposed for the replacement was a female American naval aviator Lieutenant Commander. Again, I received a frantic call from the good admiral, asking if I was trying to ruin his career. I asked for time and said I would get back to him. In researching the replacement, I found that the proposed officer was an exceptional officer who spoke fluent German. In my return call, I told the admiral about the qualifications of the young lieutenant commander and asked him to consider approving her taking the liaison position, assuring him that if I was wrong, I would personally deliver a case of good American wine to his home. Based on our mutual respect, he accepted, and the young lady worked out better than the departing officer.

This brings to mind one other German incident, in which I had taken the chairman of the Joint Chiefs of Staff, a four-star army general, to visit the USS *Independence* in the Mediterranean Sea off Naples. Following a great visit on board, we were escorted to the flight deck for a formal sendoff. Just prior to our boarding the carrier onboard delivery aircraft, the two assigned crewmembers were standing next to the boarding ladder at attention. General Brant pulled me aside and asked who the two officers were. I said that the young lady was his pilot and the young man was your copilot. He looked me straight in the eye and said, "No, she will not be my pilot." A seasoned diplomat now, I arranged to have the two switch positions.

The final incident involved once again acting as commodore on an American destroyer. Each year during Kiel Week, an American ship will transit the Kiel ship canal, which connects the Atlantic and the Baltic, cutting days off the sailing time. I had always wanted to ride a navy ship through the Kiel Canal prior to the visit for Kiel Week. In 1981, while approving the Kiel visit, I sent a message to the participating ship and asked if I could join them for their trip through the canal. They were delighted and brought me aboard at the entrance to the canal, and Franz then met me as the ship exited the canal near Kiel.

Once aboard, I was taken to the commodore's cabin, where I prepared for the evening meal. When I entered the bathroom, I found ladies' panties and bras hanging out to dry. I called the captain, and he told me that his ship had been chosen to have the first women surface warfare officers on board before there were quarters available. I said that was great but asked if she would please remove the laundry from the commodore's quarters. When I returned, the cabin was spotless with a note of apology from Lt. Patty Jones. Conversations with the ship's officers indicated she was doing a great job.

Our time in Bonn was most meaningful, and it was difficult to say good-bye to so many special friends. Probably our greatest compliment was from a German admiral who said, "If you want a great meal and prayer, you need to go to the Maxwells' home." We made the decision early on that we would pray before all meals, even when there were Soviets present. We were truly blessed with a wonderful farewell party given by Ambassador Burns and his lovely wife.

Although I knew it was going to be difficult to find a civilian position while overseas, I chose to return home and retire from the navy after twenty-seven years of service. When I reported to the Washington navy annex for retirement processing, I was asked if I wanted a formal retirement ceremony. I said, "If possible, I would like to go out the way I came in twenty-seven years ago to the day." So on December 1,1982, I reported to the navy annex, signed my retirement papers, and walked out a civilian.

My Navy awards include: Navy Commendation with combat V, Air Medal with 12 stars, Meritorious Service, National Defense Service, Vietnam Service with 3 stars, RVN Vietnam Campaign, Vietnam Cross of Gallantry, Southwest Asia Service, Cold War Victory Commemorative and Armed Forces Expeditionary.

CHAPTER 11

Time to Pray

Where does a Christian go when, in the blink of an eye, he no longer has a job? The answer is always this: to his knees.

After checking on our Springfield house in the Washington area and visiting with friends in DC, we picked up our new Mercedes Benz and, with Michael on board, headed for Missouri. Matt had just graduated from the US Naval Academy in June. Captain Matthew T. Maxwell III was privileged to swear in Ensign Matthew T. Maxwell IV. Matt was headed for navy flight school, which made your grandfather very proud. Debra had flown home ahead of us and was working in Boonville. Once home, I set up an office in my mother-in-law's basement and started sending out résumés. I was also working with headhunters in different cities. (A headhunter is a professional search firm that works with major corporations and receives a rather large sum of money from a corporation when the firm finds a position for an applicant there.)

Trent, something interesting to note is that while I was looking for a job in January 1983, we placed your dad in school at David Barton in Boonville, where you currently attend and your mom is the counselor.

As time went by and no jobs were being offered, I was becoming more concerned. Around three months after my retirement, I was contacted by a Washington, DC, search firm, asking if I was interested in working in Washington. The search firm was looking for a Washington, DC–area navy manager for the Airborne Instrument Lab Systems Corporation (AIL) on Long Island. AIL made electronics for navy and air force aircraft. My name came up because AIL manufactured the ALQ-99 system that went into the EA-6B Prowler, which I had previously flown as the commanding officer of VAQ-135, my last squadron. In addition to my military experience, I had a bachelor's degree in aeronautical engineering. I asked for a day to discuss the possibility with my family. We decided that we had nothing to lose by going through the interview process with AIL, since they would pay for my transportation to DC and Long Island.

Two days in Washington and three days at the plant gave me an excellent understanding of the requirements for the job. I felt very comfortable with the president of this multimillion-dollar company, Mr. Jim Smith. I was barely home in Missouri when the DC search firm called with an exceptional offer, stating that AIL wanted me to start as soon as possible. I thanked my contact but said I would need some time to make a decision, which did not make the headhunter very happy—I know she was already counting her bonus for her excellent find.

In past years, when we had to make major life decisions, Grandmother and I would go to the Lake of the Ozarks for some quite reflection and prayer. The following morning, we drove to the lake and stayed at the Lodge of the Four Seasons. On a blank sheet of paper, we listed all the reasons to take the job and all the reasons not to move to Washington. One of the major reasons against taking the job was that most of my work would be in the Pentagon, where I had never served during my twenty-seven-year naval career. Needless to say, much prayer went into this decision, and every day at 9:00 a.m. sharp, the search firm would call, asking if we had made a decision. I informed my contact that we were still praying about the decision, something she did not understand.

Betty and I were enjoying the lake and praying when, on the third day, the headhunter called and became very irritated with me when I advised her that I still had not reached a decision. She said she had worked for six months to fill this position and finally found a perfect fit acceptable to AIL—and here I was, praying about it. She hung up in total frustration. We decided that in fairness to the position, we should try and make a decision before our 9:00 a.m. call the next day. We asked in prayer that somehow we would know that accepting the DC position was the right move.

Late in the afternoon of the third day, a good friend I had served with in the navy found me at the lake. He had heard that I had been offered the AIL position, and since he worked in the Pentagon, he said was looking forward to working with me. Wow, God is good, and we felt this was the tiebreaker for us to seriously consider the position. After an hour on the phone with Michael and Debra, who were both very supportive, we made the decision and went out to a wonderful dinner to celebrate. The only person not very happy about our decision was Betty's mom, Grandmother Dowling. I was not concerned about my 9:00 a.m. call and thought our headhunter was going to cry when I gave her the good news.

Reflections of a Family Moving to the Big City and Starting a New Job in the Civilian World

Although our family was stationed in major cities during my navy career, we had never looked forward to living in a major city for an extended period of time. We had been told that living in our nation's capital was going to be very stressful, and we would soon find out why. I left Boonville in our new Mercedes Benz and started looking for a new home. The home we owned in Springfield, Virginia, was rented on a lease and was thus was not available for us to live in. Grandfather found a nice home in Annandale, Virginia, that was fully furnished and owned by a diplomatic couple doing a one-year overseas tour. This would give us a year to find a home while getting settled in Virginia. All of our furniture was stored, and we had a year before we would have to start paying for the storage.

Betty and Michael followed shortly. Debra was working in Boonville, so she remained with Grandmother Dowling until we found a home in Washington. Shortly after our arrival, Michael enrolled in an Annadale elementary school just a few blocks from our rented home.

We then found a wonderful real estate lady who had served with my mom and dad in the air force—another of the special God things that made our transition to Washington much easier. We found a wonderful church, Immanuel Bible Church, nearby, which also helped. Grandfather found an older two-door Oldsmobile, which the Germans would call a *strassen panzer* ("street tank") to make the forty-five-minute commute back and forth to Crystal City, near the Pentagon. Betty and Debra were slowly and with much fear learning to navigate the Washington roads and the awful beltway that completely encircled Washington.

We were truly in a new world, as I was spending long hours at the office and traveling weekly to Deer Park, Long Island, where the AIL plant was located. I would travel to the Reagan National Airport by subway and board a Delta shuttle flight to LaGuardia in New York, where I would rent a car for the one-hour drive on the Long Island Expressway to Deer Park. I would quickly learn how serious the New York City(NYC) police were about parking tickets. After I flew back to Washington on one of my trips, someone rented the car I had used from Avis. The renter then left the car parked on a New York street for three hours. When the individual did not pay the $500 fine, the police contacted Avis, who gave them my name as the car renter. Weeks later, with the fine having grown to over $3,000, the NYC police issued a warrant for my arrest. Although I had flown out of New York hours before the incident and had never been in downtown New York City, it still took the company attorneys two weeks to resolve the issue so your grandfather would not have to go to jail. Needless to say, on my future trips to Long Island—and there were many—I was very careful of where I parked.

Though very busy at work and school, we still needed to find a new home. After six months, our agent found a four-bedroom house just a block away from our current rental and directly across the street from the community swimming pool. We loved the home and would shortly sign a contract to purchase it. As with so many other events in our move to Washington, the Lord had answered our prayers. It was a glorious day when we moved in and received the delivery of our own furniture, which we had not seen for over three years.

During this time, I started volunteering with Prison Fellowship Ministries, but my involvement was reluctant at first. As mentioned earlier in my journal, in Germany in 1981, I had met Chuck Colson, CEO of Prison Fellowship. Shortly after we moved into our new house, Chuck's office called to ask if I would be interested in prison ministry. I told Chuck's secretary that I was not interested, because I was fully invested in my church and very busy at work. I also told her that the inmates had committed crimes, deserved to be in prison, and needed to do their time. Several months later, Chuck called and asked if I would at least consider taking the training for in-prison ministry. Since I had such great respect for Chuck, I reluctantly agreed to take a Saturday and go through the training. Many months after the training, the instructor from Prison Fellowship called and asked if I intended to do anything with my prison outreach training. I said I had not given it much thought. She said, "Would you consider joining a group of PF volunteers at Lorton Prison who are doing a Monday night Bible study?" A visit with my pastor, who showed me Matthew 25, convinced me to at least make one visit.

I can remember it as if it were today. Several weeks before Christmas 1983, on a freezing, black night, I sat in my car in front of Lorton Prison, where weeks ago there had been a riot, asking myself what in the world I was doing there. After a pat-down search by a male corrections officer with a metal detector, I walked through a large metal door that slammed behind me. I was instructed to go down the hill to the prison chapel. Lorton Prison sits next to a garbage dump, and the smell was putrid. I remember once again praying, "Lord, is this something you want me to do?" I recalled my pastor's encouragement from Matthew 25 and boldly stepped into the prison chapel.

The environment inside took my breath away, as I was welcomed in love by both volunteers and inmates. The one-hour worship service was probably the most authentic service I had ever attended, and I was touched more deeply than I ever had been since becoming a Christian.

Pastor George Taylor, who was the prison chaplain and would later become my mentor and teach me how to do prison ministry, brought the message. George had been the pastor of a large black church in Los Angles and had gone to prison for stealing money from the church. While serving his time, George was led to Christ by a Prison Fellowship volunteer and then joined, at the request of Chuck, the Washington PF ministry team. I can remember driving home that night, thanking the Lord for opening this ministry opportunity for me. Betty was not surprised when I told her that I learned inside the prison that except by the grace of God go I—and that I was truly hooked when I understood that our precious Lord had died not only for our sins but for the sins of the incarcerated inmates as well.

On September 18, 2013, I accepted an award for having volunteered with Prison Fellowship for thirty years. I could not help but reflect on that special evening when I had not even wanted to go inside. During special times like this, I came to better understand the true love of our Lord and Savior. From this small act of obedience grew a committed prison ministry at Immanuel Bible Church, not only inside, but also to the children of incarcerated parents through Project Angel Tree.

December 2, 1983, was a significant date for the Maxwell family. Betty, Michael, and I went to Pensacola to see Matt receive his wings of gold as a naval aviator. A very proud father had the honor of pinning on Matt's wings—the same wings I had worn for twenty-six years. Your future dad, who was a very young eleven years old, was also very proud of his brother. Matt had orders to a helicopter squadron at the naval air station in Jacksonville, Florida. One amusing incident that Matt has shared from that assignment was when he had driven to the beach to take a walk with the young lady he was dating. He parked on the beach and walked down the shore. When they returned, the tide had come in, and his new BMW was floating out to sea! He was able to retrieve the car, but the saltwater had ruined his new BMW.

In 1985, a much more significant event took place in Matt's life. He called to tell us he had met a wonderful navy widow at a Bible study and felt it was serious. Linda Reed's husband had been killed in an aircraft accident, and she had two beautiful daughters—Molly, age three, and Meghann, age seven—who truly fell in love with Matt. In September 1985, the Maxwells flew to Jacksonville for a memorable wedding on the twelfth. Molly and Meghann were just as Matt had described, precious young ladies, and your grandparents were honored to become instant grandparents.

The night before the wedding, as I drove Matt home from a bachelor party that his shipmates had thrown for him, he said, "Dad, there is something serious I must share with you. I need to tell you there will never be a Matthew Thomas Maxwell V, since Linda cannot have additional children."

I answered, "We all feel strongly that your marriage to Linda has been ordained by God, so that issue cannot be a problem."

The small but precious wedding took place the following day with two beautiful flower girls as a part of the wedding party.

While living with Grandmother Dowling in Boonville, Aunt Debra had fallen in love with Dale Windsor and, against our desires, married Dale in 1986 in Washington state. As we had feared, the marriage did not work, and in early 1987, Debra flew back to our home in Virginia. She was pregnant with Natasha, who was born at Fairfax Hospital in Virginia on August 31, 1987, as our third blessed grandchild. We have been totally blessed to have Debra and Natasha as a part of our integral family since Natasha was born.

Two years later, Michael graduated from Annadale High School. He was blessed to have his baccalaureate service at the Washington National Cathedral and graduation at Constitution Hall, also in downtown Washington. While in high school, he lettered in swimming and tennis and received good grades.

Trent, I do have to let you know that your dad did not have his own car like many of his classmates did and would not ride the school bus. When I drove him to school in my "street tank," he was so embarrassed that I would have to drop him off one block from the school so he could walk the rest of the way. He would also not let his friends ride in the car since the trunk leaked and when you turned the corner it sounded like you were in a boat. However, when driving the Mercedes Benz, I could proudly drive him up to the circle drive in front of the school. At times when we only had one car, your dad would drive the MB to school, and Grandfather would ride the bus into Washington.

Following graduation, Michael chose to attend Virginia Tech in Blacksburg, Virginia. Fun trips to Blacksburg followed with visits and football games. After Natasha was born, Debra attended secretarial school and graduated with honors. She then worked for a short time at a travel office before being hired by the Kaman Corporation, which made helicopters for the military. Her office was not far from Grandfather's office in Crystal City in Arlington, Virginia, near downtown Washington. It was great having her nearby so we could have lunch together. Debra was promoted from a small Kaman office to their main Washington office, where she became the receptionist. Senior Kaman officials often told me that Debra did an exceptional job for the company.

The family was slowly adjusting to the busyness and stress associated with Washington. Later, in 1987, I was asked to consider leaving AIL to join the headquarters staff of Prison Fellowship. While waiting for a PF offer following the interview, I was asked to consider an offer to head up the Washington office of AIL, which at the time had six employees. I was given three days to make a decision. I informed PF of my deadline and said that if I did not hear from them by the end of the third day, I was going to accept the AIL promotion. On the fourth day, PF called with an offer, which I had to turn down. We knew this was just another answered prayer for us.

Since I was the head of the Washington office, we were invited to many social events at the Kennedy Center and other very special places in DC. Two very special events among many took place. The first happened in 1987, after the Cleveland-based Eaton Corporation purchased AIL and we became the AIL division of Eaton Corporation. Eaton was and is a truck parts manufacturing firm, and there were legislative and Pentagon officials who were concerned because of the critical nature of the electronics that AIL provided to the armed forces.

To ease the concern, the Eaton leadership sent one of their senior board members to Washington to meet with congressional and Pentagon officials.

Shortly before the visit, I was informed that Eaton was sending Neil Armstrong, the naval aviator astronaut who was the first man to walk on the moon. I was asked to meet him at the Washington national airport. On the morning of the visit, Mr. Jim Smith, president of AIL, flew into Washington while I picked up Neil from the airport. I recognized Neil as he departed the aircraft, and we proceeded to my car. Once in the car, I could not believe I was seated next to a man who had walked on the moon. Neil was a very quiet, humble man of few words but had a brilliant mind. We talked about his trip down, and I shared my naval aviation career with him since we did have some things in common. We talked very little about his trip to the moon, as I was sure many others asked him extensively about his astronaut experiences. The first meeting took place in our Crystal City office, and I made sure that Michael was there and could shake the hand of a man who walked on the moon. Your future dad said he did not wash his hand for a week!

The second special visit was in 1990, following the reunification of Germany. Because I had previously been the naval attaché to Germany, Betty and I were invited to White House Rose Garden ceremony celebrating the reunification of East and West Germany. The invite was from the elder President Bush, and we were sure there would be thousands present. We arrived early and were astounded that there were less than fifty invited guests—though I believe we were outnumbered by the press. It was a beautiful program with the German ambassador and President Bush speaking about the significance of the reunification to the world. This was followed by a beautiful German youth choir, which sang both national anthems and other songs in German and English. Just before the children sang, President Bush motioned to one of his secret service agents to come and speak with him. I wondered what national or global effort the president was discussing with his agent. The agent darted off as the children sang. Following the music, the agent returned with the president's dog, Millie, for the children to see.

One other decision that we were faced with was when, in 1991, I was asked if I would consider moving to Long Island and taking over as program manager for the largest electronic program at AIL, the multimillion-dollar ALQ-99 program. This was a considerable honor and would have been a large promotion for your grandfather. Like many other things, we prayed about the offer and asked the Lord to give us a peace about this major move. Your grandparents flew to Long Island and were briefed and wined and dined by senior management. As the program manager, I felt I could do a good job of providing leadership for this very important defense contract.

We spent a day looking at homes for sale on Long Island and found them very expensive. The final night, we had a delightful dinner at the president's house, and naturally Jim Smith asked what I thought about the offer. We had an excellent discussion, and Betty and I asked if we could have some time to pray about such a significant move. I had been assured that it would not affect my Washington position if I didn't accept the offer. On the way home, we took out the yellow sheet of paper with the pros and cons on it. The tiebreakers were the cost of living in New York with just a small salary increase and the distance we would be from Michael, who was still attending Virginia Tech. Betty was wonderful about it and would have supported a yes vote if she had thought I truly wanted the position. In the end, neither of us had a peace about taking the position. Jim Smith was very gracious when I called him the following morning to decline the offer.

In late 1991, we reviewed our time in Washington and were again astounded at how we had been blessed in work, ministry, and Betty's community Bible study. We were also very blessed to attend almost yearly the National Prayer Breakfast and to be a part of the Prison Fellowship dinner the night before the event. One year, Chuck even asked me to speak after the dinner. However, despite all the blessings, Betty and I were both convinced that we did not want to grow old in the city of stress. Betty's mom's health was failing, and we had let it be known that if I could find work in central Missouri, we would consider moving home.

At the same time, Betty's brother Mike Dowling and Dave Gehm had started an environmental management company called Gehm Environmental. They had just been awarded a large state contract to administer the Missouri Leaking Underground Storage Tank (LUST) program. Mike called and asked if I would be interested in purchasing a share in the company and taking over as vice president of operations. Well, out came the yellow pad of paper and our prayer rug. After listing all of the pros and cons, we had five reasons for staying and five reasons for moving home. So, like Gideon in Judges 6:36, we decided to put out a fleece and let the Lord help us with the decision.

After talking to Debra and Michael, we had our favorite real estate lady give us a fair price for the home, and we put our house in Annandale, Virginia, on the market, deciding that if it sold for our asking price, we would move home to Boonville. However, Martha Scrabrough had advised us that it was not a good time to sell. Several months later, after many folks had looked at our house, we received an offer that was $1,000 below our asking price. Martha could not believe it when we turned down the offer. That was when we explained to Martha that the house sale at the price we had asked was our fleece for our move home. Martha was not very spiritual, and I do not think that she understood, even after reading Judges. One week later, we received a second offer by a family who loved swimming at $1,000 above our asking price. Once again, Martha was astonished.

Phone calls home accepting the Gehm Environmental offer and the submission of my letter of resignation to AIL followed. Betty flew home shortly after signing a contract on our Washington house to check on her mother and look for a new home. We departed DC with heavy hearts, because we were leaving some remarkable friends and Michael was still in school at Virginia Tech. AIL had a farewell party for us on Long Island with a very special sendoff. We left Washington with Debra and Natasha following us and met Michael in Western Virginia. So our three-car caravan continued west, with our dachshund, Gretel, riding in Michael's car, a situation she was not very happy with. At some point during the trip, Natasha switched to Michael's car, and Gretel got in the car with Debra. A few miles down the road, Debra looked in her rearview mirror to see Tasha sitting in her uncle Mike's lap, driving the car. Needless to say, Debra panicked! Fortunately, we were not near any towns, and the road was not well traveled.

The Maxwell caravan stayed together through large and small towns from Virginia to Missouri—that is, until we got to Columbia, Missouri, where Debra took a wrong turn and we lost her. With no cell phones, believe it or not, it took us a few hours to find Debra and Tasha.

CHAPTER 12

Returning Home after Thirty-Five Years

Having been home in Boonville for over twenty years now, Betty and I feel totally blessed after what has taken place in our lives. As mentioned earlier in my journal, after more than thirty-seven years away from Boonville, we would not have chosen central Missouri for our retirement years. Our personal preference would have been to retire in the Northwest near Oak Harbor, Washington, had we not felt that we needed to come home so Betty Ann could help care for her mother, Camellia Dowling. Looking back over the years, it is clear where the Lord wanted us to live.

We returned home to a wonderful house on Sonya Drive, which, for the first time in our married lives, Betty had purchased on her own without me ever seeing the house, only hearing Betty's descriptions over the phone. I went to work as vice president of operations for Gehm Environmental in a small office on Highway 87 in Boonville. When I joined Gehm, we had six employees with two working in Jefferson City with the Leaking Underground Storage Tank program, a part of the Missouri Department of Natural Resources. The main offices on Highway 87 only had two offices, and it was clear that we would need to plan for a new office in the near future. When our Gehm employees in Jefferson City took leave, I would drive there daily to fill in for our workers. I immediately learned much about the environmental business, so this was great experience.

One of our first priorities was to find a church and for me to find an accountability partner. In 1956, we had been married at the Nelson Memorial United Methodist Church here in Boonville. However, having worshipped in Washington at an independent church, we were looking for a church that was more spiritually solid than the Methodist church. As we looked, we received a call from Mrs. Lucy Farrell, whom we had known when Grandfather had attended Kemper Military School. Lucy begged us to just try Nelson Memorial UMC once. When we arrived for Sunday school, Lucy escorted us to the Challenger SS class, which was filled with solid Christian families. The lesson that day, taught by David Wrenn, was about how to know where we are being called to serve. I did not know it then, but David would later become my accountability partner, and twenty years later, we still meet weekly for accountability and Scripture memory. David and his wife, Donna, have become cherished friends. The church service that followed was worshipful and Spirit filled. We were ecstatic that we had found a church home where we were married in 1956! We would learn in the following years that Nelson was the most giving church we had ever attended.

I immediately applied to become a Missouri Department of Corrections volunteer in corrections so that I could minister at the local Boonville Corrections Center. I also immediately contacted Mrs. Janice Webb, the Missouri state director for Prison Fellowship, so that I might be involved in the state PF ministry. Betty offered to start the Nelson Memorial project Angel Tree.

Once I was cleared to work inside Boonville Corrections Center, I shared with the men an amusing story about the prison. While I was attending Kemper Military School, my family was assigned to the air defense command in Colorado Springs. Although my dad was not a pilot, he had many friends who were. On each trip east, my dad would ask the flyers to fly over and buzz Kemper after stopping at Whiteman AFB, something they were then allowed to do. After each of their flights, Dad would call to ask if we saw or heard the B-25. My answer was always no. Several months later, on a trip where the flyers brought Dad to Whiteman to visit my brother and me, he asked them if they, before landing, would buzz Kemper, and they said sure. Coming in low over Boonville, Dad looked out the window and asked the pilot, "What are you doing?" The pilot said he was buzzing Kemper. With a huge laugh, Dad finally understood why I had never seen or heard the B-25—the pilot had been buzzing the prison instead of Kemper. Dad told the pilot that the inmates must have thought that one of the ex-offenders had done well following his release.

Shortly after returning home, we learned a valuable financial lesson about how folks in the Midwest operate. As I was shopping for jeans in downtown Boonville at our friend Ed Stephens's cowboy store, Ed asked me to talk to his dad, Bud, who used to work at the Kansas City stockyards, about buying and selling cattle. Some thirty minutes later, I was fully educated on the process. A couple of weeks later, Ed called, a bit in a panic, and asked me what I had told his dad following our conversation in the store several weeks ago. I told him what he had shared was very interesting. Well, after a long pause, Ed informed me that we now owned one hundred head of cattle. My answer was that is not possible, since I had made no commitment whatsoever to any kind of deal. "Well," said Ed, "Dad understood that you would like to enter into this business deal." I then fearfully asked about my financial obligation for this deal. Ed explained that the cattle cost almost $100,000, plus $10,000 to ship them to Kansas. I told Ed, "This has to be a nightmare, since I signed no document obligating me to pay this kind of money." In a slow Missouri drawl, Ed replied, "This is how cow folks do business. You are good for the purchase, and the cattle are the collateral."

After much prayer, and being new in town, we felt obligated to stand behind the deal. The following day, Ed called to inform us that he had a bill for the first feeding in Kansas and it was for $1,400. He also informed me that for the feed bill we had to pay directly to the feedlot owner. After much prayer, we determined that the Maxwell's and the Stephens's needed to go to Kansas to verify that we truly did have one hundred head of cattle. With a ten-gallon hat (which Trent now wears) and cowboy boots, Tom, Betty, Janet, Ed's wife, and Ed headed for Kansas cow country. Many hours later, near Grand Junction, Kansas, we met the operator of the feedlot. A brief but professional explanation of the feeding operation was followed by a visit to the feedlot, where more cattle than I had ever seen in my life were fenced. We were then taken to one of the hundreds of small fenced-in areas where the Maxwell/Stephens cattle were kept. The cattle in each small feed lot were fed twice daily with food generated by a computer to fatten them up for market.

There before us were our one hundred cattle, with one lying down and not moving; the owner told us it was sleeping. Later, Ed, who knew much more about cattle, told us that cow was dead. That evening, the lot owner and his wife treated us to the best steak dinner we had ever had as he encouraged us to consider continuing to invest in his operation. The next morning, we were off over the Kansas flatlands, heading back home with a deep concern about how many more of our cattle would be lost before they could go to market. A month later, our cattle had been sold, and we both received a check that almost covered our expenses. We were later told that, if we had not lost four more cattle, we would have actually profited a little. It was a "Praise the Lord" moment in that we only lost $100, including our trip to Kansas and the cowboy hat. Needless to say, we told Ed and Bud that we were out of the cattle business. Only with someone looking over our shoulder did we not lose our shirts. We did learn a valuable welcome-to-Missouri lesson.

In Jacksonville, Matt had completed his at-sea tour and was transferred with Linda and your cousins to Virginia Beach, where Matt became the officer in charge of a drone program at Dam Neck Naval Station. Following his tour with the navy in Virginia, Matt felt that he no longer wanted to leave his family, so he retired in 1985. He served in a number of civilian positions and is now an engineer with the city of Suffox, Virginia. Following her graduation from high school, Matt and Linda's older daughter, Meghann, chose to attend Asbury College in Wilmore, Kentucky. While there, Meghann met Christopher McKnight, and we were all blessed to be a part of their precious wedding in Wilmore on July 3, 1999. Following her own high school graduation, your cousin Molly chose to attend Christopher Newport University

(CNU) in Newport News, Virginia, where she is currently a professor. Following her graduation from CNU, Molly worked at and received her PhD from Regent University in Virginia Beach. While in college, Molly met Jeremy Waters from Atlanta, Georgia, and you and your mom, dad, and grandparents were blessed to attend their wedding in Virginia Beach on October 13, 2007.

We have been totally blessed to have four precious great-grandchildren, three with Chris and Meghann and one with Molly and Jeremy. Morgan, the oldest, was born on May 21, 2003; Adeline on April 18, 2007; and Lawson on December 22, 2009. Molly and Jeremy's son, Trenton, was born on September 4, 2010. Although we have not been able to visit our Virginia family each year, we dearly appreciate the almost daily pictures our daughter-in-law Linda sends of our beautiful and growing Virginia family.

In addition to working at the BCC and with the state Prison Fellowship team, I was able to follow up with a Christian brother in Jeff City. The National Prayer Breakfast we attended each year was put on by the Fellowship, an international ministry run by Doug Coe. Prior to leaving Washington, DC, I had asked a member of Doug's staff if there were Fellowship members in Missouri. They gave me the name of Mr. Clyde Lear, the founder of Learfield Communications in Jefferson City. From our first meeting, I knew Clyde was a great brother in Christ who could help me with contacts in Missouri and with my spiritual walk. Clyde was chair of the Board of Regents at Central Methodist University (CMU), which he had attended, and additionally was the founder of the Governor's Leadership Forum in Jefferson City.

The Governor's Leadership Forum brings students from all four-year colleges and universities in Missouri to Jefferson City each January for the governor's prayer breakfast and for a leadership forum based on the life of Christ. Each group of students has an adult escort for their three days in Jefferson City, and Clyde asked your grandparents to pray about being an escort family. For five years, we had the honor of being a part of the yearly leadership forum and of fellowshipping with the Clyde Lear and his wonderful wife, Sue.

As board chair at CMU, Clyde also asked if I would serve on the search committee for a new president for the university. Six months later, we made a selection, and the board confirmed Dr. Maryanne Inman, who just retired after almost twenty years as an exceptional president. Only the Lord knew how important my affiliation with CMU and Clyde would be. The first piece of evidence that my involvement had a deeper purpose came in 1993. Michael had completed two years at Virginia Tech, but due to difficulties with his grades in such a large school, the dean had asked that your dad take a year off before returning. I was understandably upset and drove from Missouri to Blacksburg, Virginia, in order to talk with the dean. She would not talk with me until Michael gave his permission, even though I had paid all the tuition bills. I received absolutely no support from the dean and was not a happy camper. I had discussed the situation at Virginia Tech with Clyde Lear prior to leaving Missouri. He had said they would be pleased to have a Christian student transfer to CMU, so a phone call was made to Clyde, and Michael entered CMU the following fall on probation.

At Central Methodist, Michael was a stellar student and graduated with honors. After graduation, Clyde found an intern position with Learfield Communications for Michael. This was followed by a permanent position in the finance department, where he served for almost fifteen years. CMU is also where Michael met his wife.

Trent, the story of how your mom and dad met is precious. In church one Sunday, Elvin and Margene Farquhar (now your grandparents) and their daughter, your mom, sat behind your dad and his family. Your grandmother was totally mesmerized by the beauty and intellect of your mother and told me after church that we needed to have your dad ask her for a date. However, your mom had been dating a student at CMU, and your dad did not want to break up that relationship. After church the following Sunday, your grandfather Elvin came up to me and said, "The Holy Spirit told me it would be okay for Mike to ask Debbie for a date." After a number of years dating your mother, Grandmother told your dad it was time to get serious if he really loved your mom, Debbie.

Soon after that conversation, your dad asked Grandfather Elvin if he could marry your mom—but not to tell her he'd asked since he wanted it to be a surprise. On a beautiful fall evening in 1996, with a full moon, your dad took your mom to a wonderful dinner at the Plaza in Kansas City, followed by a romantic carriage ride through the Plaza, where he asked for her hand in marriage and slipped a beautiful engagement ring on her finger. Your future grandparents, knowing what was going on, also went out to dinner together, and both commented on the absolute beauty of the evening.

On July 19, 1997, in the same church Grandpa and Grandma Maxwell were married, your mom and dad had a beautiful wedding. Your mom's junior bridesmaid was your cousin Tasha, who would also be married in the same church on December 28, 2013—your grandparents' fifty-seventh wedding anniversary. Your mom's candle lighters were your cousins Meghann and Molly Reed from Virginia Beach, Virginia. Your dad's best man was your uncle Matt. In addition to the Maxwell side of the family, we were blessed to become family with the Farquhars. We dearly love our in-laws, your grandparents, Elvin and Margene.

Trent Michael Maxwell, when you were born on April 2, 2004, we were blessed again. Your dad decided to tease us when he returned from the delivery room to tell us your mom had a girl, even though the doctors had all said they were having a boy. Several seconds later, your shocked grandparents were told, "Just joking!" On that day and in so many other areas of our return to Missouri, I can see the hand of the Lord providing blessings to the family. It has been a blessing to be close enough to see you grow into a fine young man and expert fisherman, taught by your grandfather Elvin.

Gehm Environmental continued to grow and receive additional contracts. I was learning much about the environmental business, and we started to look at the possibility of federal contracts. We realized that our need for more space had only increased. A diligent search led us to a two-acre piece of property on Ashley Road that Gehm purchased in the fall of 2004. The next year, a new building was erected at 1480

Ashley Road. The new Gehm building had six private office spaces, a reception area, a kitchen, and a finished downstairs, which we rented to a counseling program. Debra joined the firm in June 1992 as the administrative manager.

Several trips to the West Coast led to contracts at the Naval Air Station Alameda, Naval Air Station North Island in San Diego, the Pearl Harbor naval submarine base near Honolulu, and Whiteman Air Force Base in Missouri. At that time, Gehm was using an electronic tool called electromagnetic offset logs (EOL) to perform site characterization for leaking underground storage tanks; it performed the job more quickly and more cheaply than drilling and sampling. As a small, veteran-owned business, we received a number of large contracts. Gehm opened a second office in Dallas in 2003 to house my brother, Jess, and Dr. Pritchard, who developed EOL. Unfortunately, there was not enough EOL business in the Dallas area to sustain the office, so after a year, it was closed but Dr. Pritchard and Jess continued to consult Gehm on EOL projects. The decision to close the Dallas office was also difficult on a personal level because it had enabled me to spend more time with my brother and his wife, Joan.

Gehm lost its contract with the Missouri DNR in 1997 when it was given to another company. Also, at that time, many sites had already been cleaned up, so Gehm's revenue was down. In 2002, I made the decision to retire from the business, which would help financially. I kept my office at Gehm and acted as a consultant when needed. I had worked for forty-two years when I finally retired. Debra remained with Gehm until the building burned in 2004. The remaining employees moved to work out of their homes, and Debra went to work for Fuqua Homes, a company that built modular homes. Aunt Debra left Fuqua homes when they declared bankruptcy in 2010 and was out of work until 2012 when she went to work as the administrator for the Nelson Memorial UMC.

In 2012, Natasha graduated from CMU, where she had been a cheerleader, and went to work as a teacher in the Head Start Program in Glasgow, Missouri. Natasha has a passion for young children and served many years as the assistant nursery director for our Nelson Memorial nursery.

Since our return to Boonville, I was blessed to not only be the lay leader in our church for five years, but also to be an active part of a growing prison ministry outreach to the local Department of Corrections Boonville Correction Center, a level-three prison (level one is minimum, and level five is maximum). In 1993, we started with the Prison Fellowship project Angel Tree, which gives Christmas gifts to children of incarcerated parents.

In 1993 there were no Angel Tree children living in Boonville, so we developed a wonderful relationship with an intercity church, Mount Zion Missionary Baptist Church, St. Louis, where many of the children lived. Betty served as the Angel Tree coordinator for Nelson UMC, and she and I have had the joy of being blessed with the Mount Zion Angel Tree coordinator, Letricia West. In addition to working with Letricia, our friendship allowed us to be with her when she lost her husband, Jerome, in 2004.

The Nelson prison outreach team has been able to build a remarkable outreach to the BCC inmates. One of our more effective programs is our annual Prison Fellowship Community Service Projects. Each September, we take eight to twelve inmates out of prison for one week to work on a community project. A home-cooked breakfast is served each morning, followed by a one-hour Christian devotion. We work together until noon, when we go to another denominational church for a home-cooked lunch. Following lunch and a short devotion by the church's pastor, we return to work. In the afternoons, student baseball players from CMU join us, and the ballplayers and inmates work alongside each other. On Sunday, the men are allowed to attend church outside the walls for the first time since they were incarcerated. The service, which you, Trent, have attended, is very special, and the men are recognized and prayed over before returning to prison. The service is followed by a celebration dinner in the Nelson Fellowship Hall. The program has been designated as a restorative justice program by the Missouri Department of Corrections.

In addition to working with our church prison outreach team, I was asked to join as deputy chair for the Prison Fellowship Missouri Ministry Team, which at the time was chaired by Roy Blunt, now a US senator. In that position, I was a part of the advisory team for our very professional PF state director, Janice Webb, on PF ministry for all twenty-one Missouri prisons. As a member of the team, in 2005, I assisted Janice in bring the PF Operation Starting Line (OSL) to seven of Missouri's prisons. OSL was an evangelical outreach that aimed to share the gospel of Jesus with as many inmates as possible. There were music groups playing worship songs and messages brought by athletes, famous singers, and talented individuals. Much travel and special visits were required to coordinate this large undertaking. I was also asked to head up an effort to look at bring the Prison Fellowship Interchange Freedom Initiative (IFI) to Missouri. IFI was a program that was charted in four states and moved inmates who had volunteered for the program into a segregated cellblock so they could be housed in a totally Christian environment. It was an eighteen-month program where, from morning to evening, the men were taught skills and teachings from a Christian prospective. During the last six months of the program, each inmate would have a Christian brother from outside the prison come in and disciple him once a week. Following release, that individual would become the ex-offender's accountability partner.

The program began in Sugarland, Texas, and the success of the IFI program, initiated while George W. Bush was governor, was well documented. With a national recidivism rate (rate of return to prison in five years) of close to 70 percent, many states were very impressed with the Texas IFI rate of less than 10 percent. I made my first visit to the Missouri Department of Corrections (DOC) in 2003 to determine whether Missouri would consider starting an IFI program in our state if the PF Missouri Ministry Team did the research. With senior DOC encouragement, Betty and I scheduled a trip to Iowa to the Newton Correction Center (NCC), the closest operating IFI program.

Our visit to NCC was one of Betty's first to a maximum-security prison, and she was very nervous. We were met with open arms by

Warden Mapes and taken to his briefing room, where his senior staff and Mr. Sam Dye, the IFI director, gave us an excellent briefing. We were then escorted through several locked doors to the IFI cellblock. I had been a prison volunteer for over twenty years, and what I witnessed in that cellblock was an atmosphere like none I had ever seen in a prison. Inmate after inmate greeted us with smiles on their faces and joy in their hearts. If you hadn't been able to see the prison walls, you would not believe you were in prison. The corrections officer (CO) on duty told me there was a large waiting list of COs who wanted to work in the IFI cellblock because there were never any kind of problems in the unit. She said she was treated with more respect from these men than from men on the street. After meeting the men, we were escorted by inmates to the IFI library and positioned at a round table with six inmates in different stages of their eighteen-month program. I learned that the Newton IFI program was the only program that allowed inmates with long sentences to join.

For the next hour, each inmate shared how IFI had changed his life. At this table, I met a devout man of God whose life had been radically changed by the love of Jesus. An inmate with many tattoos on both arms sat between Betty and me. He looked every bit like a convict. His name was Ron Gruber, and during this session, he told us that he had been the enforcer for a large motorcycle gang in Iowa and was doing fifty-eight years for second-degree murder and federal racketeering and had in a previous incarceration attempted to murder a prison CO. As the meeting progressed, Warden Mapes came into the room; standing behind Ron, the warden put his hand on Ron's shoulder. It was only later that Director Sam Dye told us that the CO whom Ron had attempted to murder was Warden Mapes and that they had reconciled. God working through the IFI program was evident, since you rarely see this type of reconciliation in a prison setting.

As we drove back to Missouri, I told Betty that this program was needed in the Missouri DOC. We then took six additional trips with DOC officials and state representatives, and all members were convinced that Missouri needed the program. State Rep. Danny Moore, who was on the committee for corrections, was our last visitor to Newton IFI, and she came away totally convinced of the need for a Missouri IFI program. A year later, an IFI program was opened at the Algoa Correctional Center in Jefferson City, and a women's IFI program began at the Vandalia women's prison.

During our six visits to Newton, I developed a brotherly Christian bond with Ron Gruber, a friendship that continues to this day. When Ron completed the IFI program, he was allowed to teach in the program— until Rev. Barry Lynn from Americans United for the Separation of Church and State sued to close the Newton IFI program. It was a sad day when the secular Iowa judge ruled to close this remarkable and effective program.

Ron now refers to me as his "zoomy brother" since he knew I had been a naval aviator. We continued to communicate via e-mail when he was moved to Rockwell City Correctional Center in Northern Iowa to serve out the remainder of his sentence. In 2011, Mark Hughes wrote a book called *Sons of Grace* that told Ron's remarkable story. Following a recommendation from your grandfather, Warden Mapes, and Mark Hughes, Ron met with the Iowa Board of Parole. Ron Gruber was released ten years early to build a new life in his new community. Now living in Northern Iowa, Ron Gruber works for Mark Hughes, distributing *Sons of Grace* to prisons throughout the United States. He also helped with the Missouri project Angel Tree in 2013.

Your grandfather was further blessed in 2012 to be able to serve as the Missouri volunteer state director (VSD) for Prison Fellowship. Due to funding issues, the Prison Fellowship state director was asked to retire, leaving no official PF presence in Missouri. Chaplain Doug Worsham, the DOC director of religious affairs, called to inform me that since PF no longer had a state director, he was going to ask his chaplains not to recognize any PF programs. Much prayer led me to volunteer to be the Missouri VSD, a role that has been a significant challenge, with twenty active prisons. Like all other areas of our lives where we are obedient to God, He allowed me to see the fruits of my labor. In September 2013, Betty and I were honored at the annual PF shining star awards ceremony in front of all the PF employees for being the Missouri VSD and having served over thirty years as a PF prison outreach volunteers. On the stage that night, I could not help but reflect on my first night at Lorton Prison in 1983. It would be exciting if I could tell you that during my thirty years, as a volunteer in many prisons, I had encountered hostage or dangerous situations, but this never occurred. I was always treated with great respect and love by our inside brothers in Christ.

Much prayer has gone into how I finish my journal to my only grandson. Through the leading of the Holy Spirit and encouragement by my special accountability partner, David Wrenn, I am going to finish with a blessed event that took place on December 28, 2013.

As I shared earlier Natasha Windsor, your cousin, our granddaughter, was married to Airman First Class Caleb Ruesing on December 28 at the Nelson Memorial UMC. Natasha has lived with your grandparents since she was born at Fairfax Hospital in Virginia, so she is more like a daughter than a granddaughter. What makes this so very special is that December 28 was the fifty-seventh wedding anniversary for your grandparents, and Tasha and Caleb were married at the same altar rail where your grandparents said their vows.

Conclusion

Dear Trent and my other wonderful grandchildren and great-grandchildren,

I want to close with the thought that your grandparents have lived a full and blessed life. The greatest blessing besides finally accepting the Lord was the gift given me of a wonderful and supportive wife of fifty-seven years. As I stood along Boonville's Main Street as Battalions Commander of the Kemper Military School Corps of Cadets, waiting for the upcoming parade, little did I know that the beautiful drum major of the Boonville High School band standing in front of the corps would be my incredible partner for life. I did not deserve your remarkable grandmother, who has been the love of my life and the most wonderful wife, mother, grandmother, and great-grandmother possible. She was the one who first introduced me to Christ, and I could not have made the journey without her. As I wrote this journal, I was totally amazed at how the Lord had worked in our lives even before we recognized Him as our Lord and Savior in June 1977 for me and in 1976 for Grandmother. If I have any regrets, it is only that I did not recognize the hand of God working in my life before age forty-two.

Trent, I deeply appreciate you encouraging me to write this journal, which has taken me over a year to complete. My prayer for all my grandchildren and great-grandchildren is that they will each have as blessed a life as your grandparents and will at a young age learn what I did not learn until later: to walk daily with Jesus. I love you all.

To honor the two hundred sixty three shipmates who gave their lives while serving their country flying the A3D Skywarrior.

Oh! I have slipped the surly bonds of Earth
And danced the skies on laughter-silvered wings;
Sunward I've climbed, and joined the tumbling mirth
of sun-split clouds,-and done a hundred things
You have not dreamed of-wheeled and soared and swung
High in the sunlit silence. Hov'ring there,
I've chased the shouting wind along, and flung
My eager craft through footless halls of air....
Up, up the long, delirious, burning blue
I've topped the wind-swept heights with easy grace
Where never lark nor ever eagle flew-
And, while with silent lifting mind I've trod
The high untre`spassed sanctity of space,
Put out my hand, and touched the face of God
By: John Gillespie Magee Jr.